Spookiest Cemeteries

Terrance Zepke

Safari Publishing

All queries should be directed to www.safaripublishing.net.

For more about this author, visit www.terrancezepke.com.

Library of Congress Cataloging-in-Publication Data

Zepke, Terrance

Spookiest Cemeteries: Discover America's Most Haunted Cemeteries / Terrance Zepke p. cm.

ISBN: 978-0-9907653-9-4

1. Ghosts-America. 2. Haunted Cemeteries-America. 3. Paranormal-America. 4. Hauntings-America. I. Title.

First edition

10 9 8 7 6 5 4 3 2 1

Cover design by Sara Whitford

Spookiest Cemeteries

About the Author

Terrance Zepke has lived and traveled all over the world during her career as a travel writer. She has been to every continent and enjoyed all kinds of adventures—from dog-sledding in the Arctic to overnight ghost investigations of some of the most haunted places in the world. She grew up in the South Carolina Lowcountry, which is full of haunted places and "haints." Terrance has a bachelor's degree in Journalism, a master's degree in Mass Communications from USC, and she studied parapsychology at the renowned Rhine Research Center. She has written close to thirty books about her favorite topics—ghosts and travel. See the back of this book for a complete list of her titles and to find out more about this author and her books. Subscribe to her *MOSTLY GHOSTLY* blog (including her annual Countdown to Halloween) and visit her **GHOST TOWN** at www.terrancezepke.com and www.terrancetalkstravel.com.

"You don't have to believe in ghosts to realize that certain places in our national history are haunted with legends and spirits of long ago... Terrance is one of the most schooled experts on paranormal in the United States."
–Rick Steves, author, national television & radio host

Introduction

If someone tells me something is "haunted," "scary," "spooky," "creepy," or "strange," I am hooked! I'm not sure why. It may have to do with my upbringing. I grew up in the South Carolina Lowcountry, which is full of Lowcountry Voodoo (more commonly known as Hoodoo), legends and lore, cemetery tours, and "haints" like Boo Hags and Bugaloos. My great aunts used to tell me the best ghost stories. I never tired of hearing about old plantations, lighthouses, cemeteries, and forts that were haunted by the likes of Civil War soldiers, lighthouse keepers, and spirits seeking lost love or retribution.

Ultimately, I wrote a book about the best ghost stories of my region, *Ghosts of the Carolina Coasts*. It is now in its eleventh printing. I wish I could take credit for it, but that rightfully goes to the ghosts found throughout these pages and beyond.

Part of the process of writing this kind of book is participating in ghost investigations (both officially and unofficially) and researching the history and hauntings of each place. Sometimes you just have to guess why a spirit lingers among the living. Other times, you have a lot more documentation to go by. But in the end, much is speculation and hearsay since witnesses are no longer alive or prove hard to locate for an interview.

But the mystery and inability to prove or disprove the supernatural is what makes these stories so compelling. Wouldn't you agree?

So read on if you want to find out why you don't

want to park in front of El Campo Santo Cemetery. Learn about the Phantom Mourners at Greenwood Cemetery, as well as the Greenwood Bride and some spooky Ghost Lights. If you end up near Resurrection Cemetery and see a female hitchhiker, be sure to stop or else you may face the wrath of Resurrection Mary.

A whole book has been written about the White Lady of Union Cemetery—and it was written by renowned demonologist Ed Warren, who happened to photograph her on more than one occasion.

But Union Cemetery does not deserve any more attention than Chestnut Hill Cemetery, which has been haunted by a vampire for more than 125 years. Or is this merely a fascinating and frightening legend?

Some of these cemeteries can be explored through a variety of interesting tour options, such as on a Segway or aboard a Tomb Buggy Tour. During this unique tour through Hollywood Forever Cemetery, you may spot celebrity spirits lurking among their graves and giant mausoleums.

Or you may have a chance to party with ghosts— if you dare. Learn where the biggest Halloween graveyard gathering is held every year and why it always ends before midnight.

Or maybe you will catch a glimpse of the very real but mysterious black-clad figure that visits Edgar Allen Poe's grave every year. Even if you don't see the Poe Toaster, the tour is worthwhile as it includes the incredibly creepy catacombs of Westminster Hall & Burying Ground. Keep your eyes open throughout this part of the tour as you may see the ghost of Poe himself.

One of my favorite stories involves a phantom farmhouse that appears and disappears right in front of your eyes at Bachelor's Grove Cemetery.

I also remain intrigued by the Voodoo Priestess, who roams St. Louis Cemetery #1 and also by Little Gracie of Bonaventure Cemetery.

One of the most haunted cemeteries dates back to the Salem Witch Trials. It also happens to be among our oldest and is located in one of the most haunted cities in America—Salem, Massachusetts.

But no cemetery has more reported paranormal activity than Gettysburg National Military Park Cemetery. During this epic three-day battle of the greatest war fought on American soil, the Battle of Gettysburg, many were mortally wounded. Thousands of men died during this battle or from injuries suffered during it. These were young men, many not even twenty years old, who surrendered their lives—not for fame or glory, but for freedom.

So turn the page and keep reading if you want to learn more about the ghosts that linger among the graves and crypts of the most haunted cemeteries in America.

Pass the Cemetery

Shadows dance across grave chilled stones
Stones shone white in rising lit moon
Moon storm shade thrill spirits
Among all marble dead that stay

—*Eve Roper*

Resurrection Cemetery

Resurrection Cemetery

Location: Justice, IL

Established: It was consecrated in 1904 and opened in 1912.

Visitor Information

Resurrection Catholic Cemetery & Mausoleum is open to the public daily from 8:30 a.m.–4:00 p.m. Monday through Friday and from 9:00 a.m.–1:00 p.m. on Saturdays. It is closed on Sundays.

If you're interested in a ghost tour of Chicago's most haunted sites, including this cemetery, you may be interested in http://chicagohauntings.com/about.html. Or you can take your own self-guided tour. Chicago Haunted Archer Avenue Tour is an audio and photo mobile tour of sixteen haunted locations on Archer Avenue and surrounding areas, including this cemetery. https://www.geogad.com/geogad/customtour?ctid=158.

It is well worth a visit even if you're not searching for paranormal activity as it has an amazing Resurrection Mausoleum. Built in 1969, this is an architectural landmark due to its faceted glass window walls, which are the largest glass installation in the world. According to *Guinness Book of World Records*, the windows measure 22,381 square feet in 2,448 panels. Also added that year was a spectacular shrine honoring Polish Christianity.

Visitors will also appreciate the Interment Chapel/Outdoor Garden Crypt Complex, which contains four chapels and more than 5,000 crypts. There are plans in the works to increase this number to 20,000 in the future. At present, there are more than 150,000 graves here.

7201 Archer Avenue
Justice, Illinois 60458 (just outside Chicago)

http://www.catholiccemeterieschicago.org/locations.php?cem=15

About the Haunted Cemetery

Resurrection Catholic Cemetery was opened in 1912 to serve the Polish Catholic community in the southwest area of the Archdiocese. Today, it serves the entire Catholic community in that area. It is also one of the largest cemeteries in America, extending nearly 550 acres.

It is also a huge draw for ghost investigators from

across the United States. Its most well-known ghost is Mary. According to legend, Mary was eighteen or nineteen years old when she was killed on her way home from the O. Henry Ballroom. The dance hall was renamed Willowbrook Ballroom in 1930.

Mary was walking home when she was killed by a hit-and-run driver. According to legend, she had stormed out of the dance hall after having an argument with her boyfriend. She was buried at Resurrection Cemetery, which is just a few miles away from the dance hall where she spent her final hours before her tragic death. She was buried in the white gown and silver dance slippers she wore that night.

Resurrection Mary, as she has come to be called, has been seen by many over the years. When the petite, blue-eyed blond-haired girl is first spotted by passersby, she is smiling and seems like a sweet girl. But if the driver doesn't slow down and offer her a ride, Resurrection Mary becomes one scary spirit. She has been known to jump on a vehicle's running boards or jump in front of the car, forcing it to stop suddenly and terrifying everyone in the vehicle.

One well-known encounter happened to Jerry (Gerald) Palus in 1939. He met a lovely petite, blue-eyed, blond-haired girl wearing a white dress and silver shoes. Gerry recalled her body and especially her hands being cold even though it was a hot night. He offered to drive her home, and Mary nodded in agreement. She remained silent during the short ride. As they passed the cemetery, she asked him to stop. He did as she asked but before he could ask her why, they were stopped at the cemetery. She said softly, "Where I'm going, you cannot follow." And with that comment, she got out of the car and disappeared just outside the cemetery gates. Jerry watched in amazement. He then hopped out and conducted a quick search while calling her name. Thinking it was not possible for her to vanish into thin air, he was sure he would find her behind a tree or hiding near the gate. But his eyes had not deceived him. She had vanished into thin air, indeed.

Sightings on Archer Street were fairly common until the 1960s when they began to be less frequent. In 1978, Shawn and Gerry Lape hit a young blonde girl, who ran in front of their car. Gerry screamed as her husband struck the girl. She stopped screaming as quickly as she had started when she realized the car had gone "through" the girl. That's when they realized she was not flesh and bone but an apparition. Turning back, they watched her disappear into the ether before their very eyes.

Sightings increased in the 1980s and 1990s when work on the cemetery was being done. One man encountered Resurrection Mary twice. He saw her on two different occasions and described her as being unusually pale and wearing a dress that had yellowed with age. She sat next to him at the dance hall but never spoke.

A cab driver stopped for her one night. She hadn't flagged him down or signaled that she needed a ride, but it was a cold night and she wasn't wearing a coat. He recalls thinking she must be in trouble being out alone on foot at night in this weather. She acted disoriented so he thought maybe she had too much to drink. She signaled him to stop in front of the cemetery, and he watched her vanish just outside the entrance gate.

And the stories go on and on of strange sightings and encounters with Resurrection Mary. The legend varies according to the source. One thing that remains consistent is reports of more than two dozen sightings during the last week of August 1980. Authorities weren't sure what to make of these reports filed by seemingly credible witnesses. The cemetery was undergoing renovations during this time so we can only speculate that this is the reason there was a spike in ghostly activity.

Sightings have been few and far between since

the early 2000s. The best chance of seeing Resurrection Mary is after 1:30 a.m. on the night before a full moon. You may see her on Archer Avenue or in the cemetery. Mary's favorite spot is near the Resurrection of Christ monument. A young woman has been seen dancing in front of the statue. If witnesses approach, she vanishes.

Another haunted place in the cemetery is the Resurrection Mausoleum. Lights, alarms, and recorded organ music go on and off for no logical reason. If you'd like to see more about Resurrection Mary you can find lots of videos on YouTube at: https://www.youtube.com/results?search_query=resurrection+mary+ghost

Colonial Park Cemetery

Colonial Park Cemetery

Location: Savannah, Georgia

Established: 1750

Visitor Information

Colonial Park Cemetery served as the city's cemetery for more than one hundred years (1750–1853). It is the oldest intact municipal cemetery in the city. The six-acre cemetery became a city park in 1896. It is open to the public. The cemetery is on the southeast corner of Abercorn Street and Oglethorpe Avenue, which is in the heart of Savannah's historic district. Before it became known as Colonial Park Cemetery, it was called the Old Brick Graveyard, Christ Church Cemetery, South Broad Street Cemetery, and Old Cemetery. The impressive arch entrance to the cemetery was added in 1913 by the Savannah chapter of the Daughters of the American Revolution.

There are several good ghost tours in Savannah and nearly all of them include this cemetery:

http://walkingtourssavannah.com/

https://ghostcitytours.com/ghosts-colonial-park-cemetery/

http://ghosttoursinsavannah.com/haunted-savannah/colonial-park-cemetery/

http://www.ghostsandgravestones.com/savannah/haunted-cemeteries.php

http://blueorbtours.com/colonial-park-cemetery/

201 E. Oglethorpe Avenue
Savannah, Georgia 31401

http://www.savannahga.gov/index.aspx?NID=879

About the Haunted Cemetery

When it was established in 1750, it was the first and only cemetery in Savannah. In a span of thirty-something years it tripled in size to encompass more than six acres. After an expansion in 1789, the graveyard was open for burial for persons of all denominations.

Dueling was a popular way to settle disputes in those days; so many dueling victims were buried here. Some headstones reveal interesting information, such as "He fell in a duel on the 16th of January 1815, by the hand of a man who a short time ago would have been friendless but for him..." (James Wilde's headstone)

When a yellow fever epidemic swept through Savannah in 1820, it claimed more than 700 lives. Most of those folks were buried in Colonial Cemetery. The cemetery closed in 1853 due to overcrowding and neglect. Laurel Grove and Bonaventure Cemeteries were established. Some families had become so distraught over the poor conditions at Colonial Park that they moved loved ones to one of these newer cemeteries. Years ago, many of the gravestones were removed.

Whatever the reason for the removal of these grave markers, there are thousands of unmarked graves, which means that visitors are literally walking on top of corpses. The yellow fever epidemic that wiped out 10 percent of the city's population in 1820 led to many being buried in mass graves. With all these mass graves and missing headstones, visitors are traipsing over the dead every time they enter Colonial Park.

During the Civil War, Union soldiers seized Savannah. They camped in the cemetery during the winter of 1864. They callously vandalized gravestones and robbed mausoleums and tombs—after removing the dead. According to some reports, soldiers removed bodies from numerous crypts so they could use them as refuge from the cold. Most likely, these bodies were reburied in a mass grave rather than returned to their original crypts—if these reports are indeed true. Talk about disturbing the dead.

The city nearly tore down the cemetery but a lawsuit by Christ Church stopped that from happening. It is unclear what the city was going to do with all those interred here but surely they weren't planning on building on top of all those graves? Thankfully, we'll never know. The court forced the city to protect and convert the old cemetery into a public park. By the late 1800s, benches and paths had been added throughout the grounds. This was a good start but hardly enough to placate the poor souls who had been disturbed from their final resting spot or who had been quickly disposed of in a mass, unmarked grave.

Much later, markers were made by the Georgia Historical Commission and placed beside graves denoting important individuals or events.

We'll never know just how many ghosts haunt this place and why, but we do know the ghost of Renee Rondolia Asch (or Rene Asche Rondolier, according to some sources) can be found here. Renee had a lot of strikes against him. He was an orphan, he was disfigured, and he had some serious mental health issues. According to legend, he killed small animals just to watch them die. And he liked to hang out in the cemetery.

So when two young girls were found dead in the cemetery, townsfolk became convinced that Renee killed them. He was lynched in the swamp not far from the cemetery. After Renee's death, more victims were discovered in the cemetery. Was it possible that Renee killed those girls? Maybe it had been someone else. The townspeople didn't entertain that thought. They believed they had done what needed to be done. Never mind a trial or evidence. Folks also felt sure that the spirit of Renee was exacting his revenge. Some even refer to the cemetery as "Renee's Playground."

There was a woman who worked as a maid at the City Hotel. One night, when she finished her shift and started home, she ended up walking a few yards behind a man who had left the hotel at the same time. She assumed it was a guest out for a late night stroll. She was shocked when he literally disappeared at the gates of Colonial Park Cemetery.

Footage of a child running through the cemetery has been captured by a visitor. The boy seemed to float up into a tree and then out of it before vanishing. I've seen this film clip, and I can't say for sure what it is. It is possible it is a ghost. You can decide for yourself by watching the video, which has been posted on YouTube:
https://www.youtube.com/watch?v=C38ZvJjqX4c.

WHO'S BURIED HERE?

Lots of famous folks have been laid to rest here, such as Button Gwinnet, who was a signer of the Declaration of Independence. James Habersham, who was the Acting Royal Governor of the Providence from 1771–1773 is interned here. Samuel Elbert, who was a Revolutionary War soldier and Governor of Georgia, Archibald Bulloch (First Governor of Georgia) and Lachlan McIntosh (Major General of the Continental Army) are buried here. Major General Nathanael Green was buried here before being reinterred in Johnson Square in 1901.

Archaeologists have discovered nearly 8,700 unmarked graves in addition to the more than 550 marked graves.

FYI: The American Institute of Parapsychology ranks Savannah as the most haunted city in America. It's no wonder since it is a city literally built upon its dead. The great fire of 1820 claimed many lives. Remarkably, that same year a yellow fever epidemic claimed thousands. With so many deaths, it was overwhelming. Bodies were disposed of in some unusual ways and mass graves were dug all over the place. In addition to Bonaventure and Colonial Park cemeteries, Savannah is full of other haunted places including Pirates' House, Hampton-Lillibridge House, Mercer House, 17Hundred90Inn, and Sorrel Weed House. There are many options for exploring the haunted side of Savannah, such as hearse tours, doomed trolley rides, and cemetery walks.

www.savannahvisit.com

St. Louis Cemetery #1

St. Louis Cemetery #1

Location: New Orleans, Louisiana

Established: 1789

Visitor Information

The cemetery sits on the peripheral of the French Quarter, just eight blocks from the Mississippi River. It closes promptly at 3:00 p.m. during the week and is only open until noon on the weekends. It is owned and maintained by the Archdiocese of New Orleans. Recently, they changed the rules for visitation. All visitors must be accompanied by a tour guide and pay a fee to enter the cemetery. Even family members with loved ones buried here must receive permission to visit.

A non-profit group, Save Our Cemeteries, offers tours and is one of the best ways to explore this historic cemetery: www.saveourcemeteries.org. There are some other options too:

https://www.frenchquarterphantoms.com/cemetery-tour

http://magictoursnola.com/tours/cemetery-tours

http://www.freetoursbyfoot.com/new-orleans-tours/walking-tours/st-louis-1-cemetery-tour/

If you visit, you may wish to follow a longtime tradition. According to legend, if you make a wish after knocking three times on the front of Marie's tomb, leaving an "XXX" in chalk (you'll see where others have done this) and then knocking again three times, whatever you wish will come true. To be certain of this, it is advisable to leave an offering, such as flowers, coins, charms, or candles. You will see where many others have done this ritual.

The removal (or even moving) of objects inside a New Orleans cemetery is punishable by law. This is considered a serious offense and witnesses are encouraged to phone the police. Visitors are asked to be respectful of the dead when inside the cemetery and not to litter, vandalize, or act inappropriately.

499 Basin Street
New Orleans, Louisiana 70112

http://www.neworleansonline.com/directory/location.php?locationID=1945

About the Haunted Cemetery

More than one hundred thousand people have been buried in this cemetery that is only one square block in size. This is one of three cemeteries that make up the St. Louis Cemetery. It has survived fires, floods, neglect, and vandalism. It is also the oldest surviving cemetery in New Orleans, dating back to 1789, which makes it historically important. It is on the National Register of Historic Places.

St. Louis Cemetery was built to replace St. Peter Cemetery, which no longer exists. The graves are all built above ground because the city is below sea level. Visitors will note that the few existing old slab graves have been weighted down with bricks so that coffins do not pop up out of the ground.

A major fire, yellow fever epidemic, and flood in the late 1800s results in so many deaths that the bodies were often lying around for days waiting for graves to be dug. According to legend, gravediggers stayed intoxicated so as to tolerate the stench from the decaying bodies.

Interestingly, during the immense flooding that followed Hurricane Katrina, the cemetery remained unscathed. No tombs were damaged. The only indication of the legendary flood is the waterline marks that can be seen on most tombs.

The vaults vary according to affluence. Some are quite simple while others are very ornate. Some are very small and some big enough to accommodate a large family. Some family tombs look like cute, little houses surrounded by iron fences. You may hear folks refer to the tombs as "ovens." That's because many of them are shaped like old-timey brick ovens.

At the back of the cemetery is pauper's field. This is a large area with unmarked graves for folks who cannot afford to buy a vault. Even those who could not afford a vault could usually find a family who would allow them to be added to their vault rather than be buried in pauper's field.

Tombs are generally constructed of brick and covered with stucco or plaster. They are usually parapet or platform tombs. Their conditions vary from derelict to good, depending on upkeep and restoration efforts. Some vaults were valuable and as such were deed in wills and sold during tough economic times.

Some of the tombs were stolen by unscrupulous people. A man named Henry Vignes had the deed to his family's vault. He left the papers with his landlady when he went to sea, trusting her to keep them safe. Instead, she sold the vault for a tidy sum. When Henry came home, he discovered he no longer owned the vault. Sadly, before the matter could be resolved, Henry died. He was buried in pauper's field in an unmarked grave.

Since this is a Roman Catholic cemetery, Jews and Protestants were buried in the back of the cemetery so as to separate them from the Catholics. One of the most distinguishing things about the cemetery is the several alleys and paths that wind through and around the vaults. They vary from itty-bitty alleys to wide pathways.

Many notable citizens are buried in the six-hundred-plus tombs found here. For example, Paul Morphy (world champion chess player), Etienne de Bore (first mayor of New Orleans and successful entrepreneur), Bert Brigand Lagon (former city planner who joined Jean Lafitte's pirate crew), and Bernard de Marigny (President of Louisiana Senate). Marigny is credited with bringing the game of craps to New Orleans. He also gambled all his money away and had to sell off his family plantation. He died a pauper.

However, there is no doubt who is the most famous inhabitant of this cemetery. It is Voodoo Priestess Marie Laveau. She was conceived when a plantation owner and a Creole woman had a brief affair. She married when she was barely eighteen years old, anxious to start a better life. She married a Haitian man who introduced her to voodoo, which is called "Santeri" in Haiti.

Laveau became known as New Orleans's greatest voodoo priestess during the 1800s. She created powerful potions and charms.

She worked as a hairdresser and helped the afflicted during several epidemics. She had a daughter whom she named Marie. She taught her daughter everything she knew about voodoo. Both women had quite a following. In fact, when the senior Marie died, she was not allowed to be buried in her family's vault. Authorities feared that her followers would besiege the cemetery and cause disruption. So she was buried in an unmarked grave. Her powers were believed to be so great that she still possesses them in the afterlife. This is why visitors often bring gifts to be placed in front of her tomb along with their requests.

Oddly, the same authorities allowed her daughter, Marie Deux, to be buried in the family vault. Perhaps, they realized they had no legal right to stop her. Or maybe they were fearful of retribution by the priestess and her followers.

Some of the folks buried here are the ones who haunt it. These spirits have been seen by visitors and appear more human than apparitions in appearance. The spirit of Henry Vignes approaches visitors and asks for assistance finding his family's vault. He sometimes appears during a funeral service.

Many believe Marie Laveau and her daughter haunt the cemetery. Being forbidden a proper burial would certainly be reason enough for Laveau's spirit to linger. She is seen on a path near her family's vault. Perhaps she is trying to find a way in or simply stay close to her family. She has cursed visitors but does not follow when they leave to get away from her.

The spirit of a man named Alphonse has been known to touch visitors. He extends an icy hand either on a shoulder or when he grips a visitor's hand in greeting before disappearing. He always disappears after making contact. He is seen on occasion bringing flowers to graves.

Investigations have shown shadowy figures and orbs in photographs and strange EVPs have been recorded. One recording reveals *"I need to rest!"*

New Orleans has forty-two cemeteries scattered throughout the city. Dubbed "Cities of the Dead" these graveyards are so crowded that visitors have been known to get lost among the many vaults and alleys.

The dead outnumber the living in New Orleans.

New Orleans, also known as The Big Easy, Crescent City, and NOLA, is one of the most haunted cities in America, presumably because there are more dead than living.

Most of the city is below sea level, which is why there are so many tombs rather than graves.

There's a video tour of this cemetery that includes an EVP believed to be Marie Laveau. Watch and listen carefully:
https://www.youtube.com/watch?v=Nob2DDQELVI

Marie Laveau has been a New Orleans icon since 1988.
Located at 739 Bourbon Street (French Quarter).
Visitors will find everything from T-shirts to tarot
cards.
www.voodooneworleans.com

Bonaventure Cemetery

Bonaventure Cemetery

Location: Savannah, Georgia

Established: Circa 1846

Visitor Information: Perched on the east end of Savannah overlooking the Wilmington River, this 100-acre cemetery is open to the public during daylight hours. It is a lovely place filled with ancient oaks, blooming azaleas and roses, and intriguing sculptures of angels and cherubs. It was private until 1907 when it became a public cemetery. It remains one of the largest municipal cemeteries in the city. The deceased are still being buried at Bonaventure.

Here are some tour options that are available:

www.ghostsandgravestones.com

http://6thsenseworld.com/bonaventure-cemetery-tours

http://www.viator.com/Savannah-tours/Ghost-and-Vampire-Tours/d5166-g4-c118?pref=204

330 Bonaventure Road
Savannah, Georgia

http://www.savannahga.gov/?nid=864

About the Haunted Cemetery

Colonel John Mullryne and his wife Claudia bought a 600-acre tract of land in 1762. They named their plantation, Bonaventure, which means "good fortune." Oddly, no crops were ever planted here. Instead, oak trees were planted every fifteen feet along the "roads" of the property.

John's youngest daughter, Mary, married Josiah Tattnall. They had two children, John Mullryne Tattnall and Josiah Tattnall Jr. During the Revolutionary Way, Royal Governor James Wright eluded capture by hiding out at Bonaventure. French troops arrived in Savannah via the St. Augustine creek, which was behind the plantation in 1779. French troops used the plantation as a hospital during the Siege of Savannah. The new government commandeered the property in 1782 and sold it at a public auction. It was bought by a friend of the Tattnell family, John Habersham, who sold it to Josiah Tattnall Jr. and his wife Harriet.

The couple had nine children at Bonaventure from 1786 to 1801. Josiah served as governor of Georgia. Harriet died in 1803 and her husband died the following year. Josiah, Harriet, and four of their nine children are buried at Bonaventure. The orphaned children were raised by grandparents in London. Josiah Tattnall III, who became a commodore in the Confederate Navy, sold the property to Peter Wiltberger in 1846.

Wiltberger used seventy acres to establish the Evergreen Cemetery Company of Bonaventure, which was designed around the ruins of the Tattnell house. The first house burned down in 1771 and the second house was destroyed in the early 1800s.

There's a great story about Josiah and his last night in this house. Josiah loved to entertain and often had a houseful of guests. One night, he was throwing one of his lavish parties when the house caught fire.

When the servants notified Josiah of the fire, he calmly told them to start taking the food and chairs out onto the lawn. Shocked but obedient, the servants began running back and forth carrying large platters of food, a table, and chairs. After the party had been relocated outdoors, the servants were instructed to try to extinguish the fire.

The Tattnalls and their guests, garbed in formal attire, sipped cocktails as they watched the men try to put out the fire. As anticipated, the fire spread rapidly through the wooden house, rendering their efforts useless. The group assembled on the lawn continued to party, illuminated by the fire that ultimately consumed Bonaventure Plantation.

Some question this story, but there is no evidence to dispute it and the fire is well documented.

FYI: Some of the famous folks buried at Bonaventure include singer/songwriter Johnny Mercer, Governor Edward Telfair, Confederate General Hugh W. Mercer, Bishop Middleton Barnwell, actor James Neill, and poet Conrad Aiken.

Several prominent families transferred the remains of their loved ones from other cemeteries to Evergreen. Peter Wilberger's wife, Susan, was the first burial that was not a transfer from another cemetery. Peter was buried beside his wife in 1853.

The city of Savannah bought the cemetery in 1907 and changed the name to Bonaventure Cemetery. In 2001, Bonaventure Cemetery was placed on the National Register of Historic Places.

A stop at the cemetery is included on most ghost walks and an evening of storytelling is held seasonally because the place is haunted by several spirits.

One of these spirits is believed to be Josiah Tattnall, who is buried here. A figure has been seen near his grave wearing formal attire from that era. Also, the sounds of party (laughter, glasses clinking, and music) have been heard on occasion near Tattnall's grave. Perhaps, Josiah Tattnall still enjoys a good party.

The most famous ghost of Bonaventure Cemetery is Little Gracie. She was born in 1883 and died just six years later of pneumonia. Her father was the manager of the Pulaski House, which was one of the best hotels in Savannah at that time. He was devastated by the loss of his only child. His love and great sorrow is immediately apparent to all who visit the cemetery. They will see a large lifelike statue that marks her grave. It so closely resembles her—right down to the details of her dress, her chubby cheeks, and adorable pigtails. The exquisite marble statue was made by well-known sculptor, John Waltz, who used a photo to create the statue.

Over the years, visitors have left lots of little toys

around the statue and gravesite. Some swear to have seen tears of blood coming out of the eyes of the Little Gracie statue when any of these toys are removed. Even odder if it is to be believed, is the coin trick. According to legend, if you place a coin on top of the downturned hands of the Little Gracie statue and then circle the statue three times, the coin will disappear. There is no way to test if this is true since the grave is now fenced off. The fence had to be added to protect the statue once the rumor circulated that rubbing the statue brought good luck. All the rubbing led to harming the delicate marble. There have also been reports of children playing and crying in this part of the graveyard.

A young woman named Corinne committed suicide and was buried here. She has haunted the cemetery for decades. She is seen near her grave wearing a sad smile and gesturing. There has been much speculation as to whether she is pointing or waving or signaling, perhaps trying to get visitors to join her?

There have also been reports of phantom dogs and shadowy figures that disappear when visitors try to approach them.

FYI: Many mistakenly believe the Bird Girl Statue, made famous by the book and movie, *Midnight in the Garden of Good and Evil,* is in Bonaventure Cemetery. It was removed many years ago and placed in the Telfair Museum of Art in order to protect it. You should read this book or watch the movie if you haven't done so already. The story is based on remarkable real life events and quirky real life residents of Savannah.

Bachelor's Grove Cemetery

Bachelor's Grove Cemetery

Location: Chicago, Illinois

Established: 1845

Visitor Information

This cemetery is not open to the public. There is a chain-link fence around it to protect it from vandals, but they have accessed it anyway by cutting holes in the fence. Additionally, fallen trees have damaged the fence. There is no longer a sign denoting the cemetery but there is a "No Trespassing" sign posted. Furthermore, the cemetery is not accessible by vehicle. There is only a path for foot traffic.

The cemetery is on the southwest edge of Rubio Woods Forest Preserve, which is on the southwest side of Chicago at Midlothian. The only safe place to park your vehicle is in the parking lot of the preserve. Since the preserve is only open during daylight hours, you should plan to visit (and park in this lot) during the day. The wooded area where the path begins is called Everdon Woods. Look for the "Everdon Woods" sign to find the entrance to the path. I am not encouraging trespassing, but for those who ignore the warnings, please be respectful of the dead and do not vandalize the cemetery or be disrespectful in any way. Also, be aware that trespassing is against the law.

143 Street (just east of Ridgeland Avenue)
Chicago, Illinois 60445

FYI: The one-acre cemetery has also been known as Bachelor Grove, Batchelor Grove, Batchelder's Grove, and Everdon.

About the Haunted Cemetery

Bachelor's Grove community was established in the 1830s by British migrants from New England. The settlement began with four single men, hence the name "Bachelor's Grove." (Note: Some claim it was Barchelder, not Bachelor, and that Grove was the name of a family who settled here in the 1840s.) The cemetery began as a burial ground for this early settlement.

Although there have been no burials here since 1965—or to be accurate, it would be 1989 if you count *ashes* buried at Bachelor's Grove—paranormal activity continues to be reported. There have been more than a hundred documented reports filed.

It's no wonder that the spirits of those buried here are restless. There has been a lot of disturbing the dead. For example, there has been a great deal of vandalism since the cemetery closed. Reportedly, there were more than two hundred tombstones and now there are less than twenty. This means that only two dozen grave markers have not been vandalized. One report contradicts this by indicating that bodies that have not been stolen have been moved to other area cemeteries by family members. If this is true, this may explain what has happened to so many of these grave markers. Presumably, the family also removed the gravestones. So it is impossible to determine if there are any bodies left in this abandoned cemetery or how many markers were legitimately removed or simply stolen over the years.

We do know for sure that some graves were dug up by looters. Yes, this means that coffins *and* corpses were stolen—talk about disturbing the dead.

To add insult to injury, satanic rituals have taken place here, as well. These ceremonies include black magic, damaging trees and gravestones with strange inscriptions, and animal sacrifices. Park rangers and cemetery visitors have found the bones of chickens and cats scattered around the cemetery.

There have been numerous investigations over the years by reputable groups, including Ghost Adventures and Ghost Research Society. They have found evidence to support a variety of paranormal activity, such as:

Woman on a Tombstone

There was nothing there when the photo was taken, but when developed, a woman sitting on a grave was clearly visible. The photo, taken by Ghost Research Society (and proven not to have been altered in any way) ran in the *Chicago Sun-Times*. It shows a translucent woman sitting atop a granite grave marker. This is not an orb or indeterminable shadowy figure but quite clearly a young lady wearing an outdated or vintage dress.

White Lady

A woman is seen near a child's grave wearing a long white dress that sort of looks like a gown or robe. The best chance of seeing her and the baby she is carrying is when the moon is full. It is believed she and the baby died during childbirth or soon thereafter. Some claim to hear a baby crying and see a woman in white but no baby. The White Lady is also known as the Madonna of Bachelor's Grove because of the snow-white gown she wears.

Phantom Farmhouse

Perhaps, strangest of all is this sighting. Witnesses report seeing a small, traditional farmhouse that vanishes as they go toward it to investigate. This was often reported during the 1950s. It was seen during the day and at night and appeared during many different weather conditions so there didn't seem to be any pattern to the sightings.

Ghost Lights

Orbs have appeared on numerous photos taken in the cemetery. The lights are seen along the trail to the cemetery and have been reported as reddish in color.

Ghost Plow

There is a pond (pictured here) adjacent to the cemetery. A glowing aura has been reported coming off it late at night. A man, horse, and plow have been seen disappearing into the woods or into the water. It is presumably a farmer, or is it? According to legend, this body of water was used as a dumping ground by the mafia in the 1960s. Could what these folks are seeing be the spirit of the man charged with disposing the bodies rather than a farmer?

Monk

Some witnesses claim to have seen a figure wearing what appears to be the traditional robe with hood that is worn by monks. No sightings have been reported of these spirits since the 1980s.

Ghost Dog

A phantom dog has been seen near the entrance to the cemetery. When this black dog is approached by visitors, the animal disappears before their very eyes. No sightings have been reported since the 1990s.

FYI: There is a 75-minute documentary posted on YouTube that details some ghost investigations and offers a good look inside the private cemetery: https://www.youtube.com/watch?v=stQizIlmKaU

Gettysburg National Military Park Cemetery

Gettysburg National Military Park Cemetery

Location: Gettysburg, Pennsylvania

Established: Construction began in 1865 and there was a dedication ceremony in 1869, but the cemetery was not completed until 1872.

Visitor Information

The roughly 6,000-acre Gettysburg National Military Park is open year-round from sunrise to sunset except on Thanksgiving, Christmas Day, and New Year's Day. Visitors can explore independently or take a guided tour. Special events and ranger programs are offered seasonally. The best place to start is the visitor's center, which offers two special options: the Gettysburg Cyclorama and a twenty-minute film narrated by actor Morgan Freeman. There is also a gift shop and Refreshment Saloon.

Additionally, the museum features one of the largest collections of Civil War relics in the world, as well as twelve museum galleries. The seventeen-acre Soldiers National Cemetery and the David Wills House are part of this park.

More than one million people visit annually, making it one of the most visited parks in America. There are 1,328 memorials, monuments, and markers throughout the park, which gives it the distinction of having the largest outdoor collection of sculptures in the world.

There are several tour options.

Self-Guided. You can explore on your own or there is a free video tour available online. It can be accessed on a mobile device at each designated stop. The average running time is four minutes.

http://housedivided.dickinson.edu/sites/civilwar/gettysb
urg-virtual-tour/

Walking Tours. These ninety-minute historic tours are
led by licensed, expert guides.
http://www.civilwar.org/civil-war-discovery-
trail/sites/gettysburg-guided-historic-walking-
tours.html

Car & Bus Tours. Licensed Battlefield Guides train
for years and must pass extensive tests administered by
the National Park Service to qualify to give tours. There
are two options for touring—privately in your own car
or by bus.
http://www.gettysburgfoundation.org/14/gettysburg-
battlefield-tours

Ghost Tours. There is even the option to participate in
an official ghost investigation.
http://www.gettysburgtours.net/offer/17196/Gettysburg
-Paranormal-Investigation#.VrQPY4-cGUk

http://gettysburgghosttours.com/

http://ghostsofgettysburg.com/

http://gettysburgparanormalinvestigations.com/gettysbu
rgghosttours.htm

http://www.farnsworthhouseinn.com/ghost-tours.html

Special Programs. Aside from a battlefield tour, there are many other things to see and do including free ranger-guided programs, evening campfire programs, activities for kids, and specialized battle walks during the summer months.
http://www.nps.gov/gett/planyourvisit/things2do.htm

1195 Baltimore Pike (visitor's center)
Gettysburg, PA 17325

www.nps.gov/gett

Parking for the cemetery, which is adjacent to the visitor's center, is a lot located between Taneytown Rd. and Steinwehr Ave. (Bus. Rt. 15)

http://www.nps.gov/nr/travel/national_cemeteries/Pennsylvania/Gettysburg_National_Cemetery.html

FYI: Civil War-related sites that are located near the Gettysburg National Military Park & Soldiers Cemetery include Harpers Ferry National Historical Park, Antietam National Battlefield, and the Monocacy National Battlefield. All of these, except Monocacy, are also reportedly haunted.

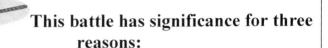

This battle has significance for three reasons:

*It was the largest battle fought in North America.

*It was the bloodiest battle of the Civil War with 51,000 killed, wounded, missing, or captured.

*It was considered "The High Water Mark of the Rebellion."

About the Haunted Cemetery

To understand all the paranormal activity you must first understand what happened here. It all began after General Robert E. Lee won the Battle of Chancellorsville. This motivated him to pursue a second invasion of the North, which was known as the Gettysburg Campaign. Major General George Meade's army met up with Lee's army just north of Gettysburg on July 1, 1863. Reinforcements arrived for both sides and the fighting continued into July 2. Heavy fighting took place throughout the day all over the area, including McPherson's Ridge, Oak Hill, Oak Ridge, Seminary Ridge, Barlow's Knoll, and in the town of Gettysburg.

The second day of the Battle of Gettysburg was the longest and costliest of this three-day battle. It took place at Devil's Den, Little Round Top, the Peach Orchard, the Wheatfield, Cemetery Ridge, Trostle's Farm, Culp's Hill, and Cemetery Hill. Approximately 100,000 soldiers were engaged in combat on July 2 and more than 20 percent of those men were dead, wounded, captured, or missing by the end of the day. This was one of the top ten bloodiest battles of the whole war. Day three (July 3) was the last day of this historic battle. It culminated with the famous Pickett's Charge. The Confederacy attempted to break the Union line at Cemetery Ridge.

Roughly 12,000 Confederate soldiers charged the Union line. They were unsuccessful and suffered heavy casualties. General Lee had no choice but to beat a hasty retreat back to Virginia. The loss of this important battle was a turning point in the War Between the States. It was the beginning of the end for the Confederacy.

FYI: There were 120 generals at the Battle of Gettysburg. Nine died during the battle or as a result of battle wounds.

Soldiers National Cemetery

Since this was the bloodiest battle of the entire war, it is certainly not surprising that this is one of the most haunted battlefields and cemeteries in America. In fact, the hauntings extend well past the park. They are all over town of Gettysburg since the three-day battle was fought in several different areas. Over the years, there have been many reports of paranormal activity, such as encounters with soldiers' spirits and inexplicable sounds of artillery fire and battle cries. The most haunted places within the park are at Little Round Top, Slaughter Pen, and Devil's Den.

If you want to hear stories about these hauntings, you need to hire a guide as the park rangers won't talk about them. They have been instructed not to although several former rangers have been candid about the paranormal encounters they had while working at the park. According to legend, Devil's Den was haunted long before the bloody battle that took place on the second day of the Battle of Gettysburg. If it wasn't haunted before, it certainly was after this skirmish. Confederate corpses were left to rot for days, possibly weeks. Some may never have been buried but simply tossed into the deep crevices within Devil's Den. The spirit of a Texan soldier has been seen on many occasions.

Other parts of the park that are well-known to be haunted include the Soldier's Cemetery, George Weikert House, Hummelbaugh House, and Rose Farm.

The most haunted places outside the battlefield are Gettysburg College, Cashtown Inn, Jennie Wade House, and the Farnsworth House Inn. Twenty-year-old Jennie Wade was the only civilian casualty of the Battle of Gettysburg. She was killed when a musket ball smashed through her door, killing her instantly. Residents, realizing they could suffer the same fate, soon left their homes.

Soldier's National Monument

Visitors can see all the bullet holes that riddle the walls of Farnsworth Inn. One of the rooms has been padlocked to prevent anyone from entering. It was here that a couple of Confederate sharpshooters were posted. It is believed that one or both must have suffered a severe injury or possibly was killed in this room. The spirit or spirits that appear are considered to be mean spirits. There are several other haunted areas within the Farnsworth House.

Gettysburg College's Pennsylvania Hall was used as a field hospital and lookout post. Over the years, there have been numerous reports by staff and students who swear they have seen soldiers in the building's cupola as if on sentry duty. Yet, whenever anyone, such as faculty or security, goes to investigate, they do not find anyone in or around the cupola.

There is one story that is quite disturbing if it is to be believed. One night, two women who worked in the administrative office were working late. When they finally finished up, they took the elevator down to the main level as usual. However, the elevator did not stop on the first floor but descended to the basement, which had served as the operating theater during the war. The doors opened and revealed a horrifying sight. It looked as if they had stepped back in time to when it had been an operating area. It was a very chaotic scene filled with nurses scurrying around and bodies and blood everywhere. Surgeons wearing bloody aprons could also be seen. One of them looked up and gestured for them to come and help. They screamed and frantically punched the elevator button, which ascended to the first floor. Both women continued to work for the school but refused to ride the elevator or work late after that night.

 About the Gettysburg Address

This was a short speech given by President Abraham Lincoln (pictured here) on November 19, 1863 when the Soldiers National Cemetery was dedicated. This was just a few months after the Battle of Gettysburg. It is considered to be one of the greatest speeches in American history.

The Gettysburg Address

Four score and seven years ago our fathers brought forth on this continent, a new nation, conceived in Liberty, and dedicated to the proposition that all men are created equal.

Now we are engaged in a great civil war, testing whether that nation, or any nation so conceived and so dedicated, can long endure. We are met on a great battlefield of that war. We have come to dedicate a portion of that field, as a final resting place for those who here gave their lives that that nation might live. It is altogether fitting and proper that we should do this.

But, in a larger sense, we cannot dedicate—we cannot consecrate—we cannot hallow—this ground. The brave men, living and dead, who struggled here, have consecrated it, far above our poor power to add or detract. The world will little note, nor long remember what we say here, but it can never forget what they did here. It is for us the living, rather, to be dedicated here to the unfinished work which they who fought here have thus far so nobly advanced. It is rather for us to be here dedicated to the great task remaining before us—that from these honored dead we take increased devotion to that cause for which they gave the last full measure of devotion—that we here highly resolve that these dead shall not have died in vain—that this nation, under God, shall have a new birth of freedom—and that government of the people, by the people, for the people, shall not perish from the earth.

**"Hancock at Gettysburg" by Thure de Thulstrup
(Pickett's Charge)**

Quite a bit of paranormal activity has been reported in the Gettysburg National Cemetery. One of the most haunted areas is Cemetery Lodge. This building once housed the personal possessions of soldiers killed during the Battle of Gettysburg that had not been claimed by family. Even though these items are no longer stored here, reports keep coming in about footsteps and muffled voices being heard when no one is inside. Witnesses say it sounds like boots going up the stairs. Upstairs is where the personal effects were once stored. The lodge is at the entrance to the Gettysburg National Cemetery, near the intersection of Baltimore Pike and Emmitsburg Road.

On Cemetery Ridge, near the Pennsylvania Monument, Civil War band music is often heard. No source has ever been discovered or logical explanation given for this phenomenon.

The spirit of Captain William Miller used to haunt the cemetery. A psychic was brought to the cemetery to hopefully find out why. It was revealed to the psychic that Captain Miller had been awarded a Medal of Honor but this was not included on his tombstone. When this error was corrected, the hauntings stopped.

Some visitors have seen orbs or unidentifiable images on their photographs once developed. Some have recalled feeling nauseous or like they were being watched by an unseen presence. A few have claimed they heard identifiable sounds, such as shouts, cries, and whispers. Of course, this could just be their imagination or it could be something supernatural.

Westminster Hall Burying Grounds & Catacombs

Westminster Hall Burying Grounds & Catacombs

Location: Baltimore, Maryland

Established: 1786 (The church was not built until 1852.)

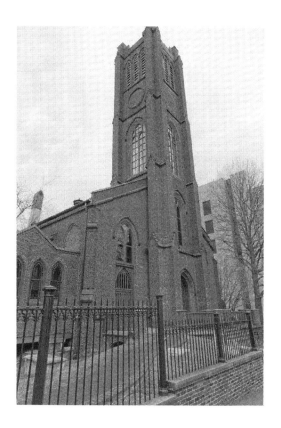

Visitor Information

Also known as Westminster Presbyterian Churchyard, the cemetery is open to the public from 8:00 a.m. to dusk daily. Visitors are welcome to take self-guided tours, which include information plaques throughout the property. Additionally, guided tours are held on select days of the week. Private tours can be arranged.

There is an annual Halloween Tour that takes place on October 31. No reservations are required but there is a fee for children and adults. Creepy music is played on Westminster's 1882 organ. Readings and performances of Edgar Allan Poe's best stories are given, as well as tours of the church and burying ground which includes 180 graves and catacombs.

519 W. Fayette Street (in downtown Baltimore at intersection of Fayette and Green Streets)

Baltimore, Maryland 21201

www.westminsterhall.org

While in Baltimore, you may want to visit the Poe House Museum: www.epoe.org.

Some say Poe's house, now a museum, is also haunted.

About the Haunted Cemetery

The graveyard was established roughly sixty years before the church was built. So as not to disturb the graves, the edifice was built on top of brick piers. It is unclear as to why the church had to be built on top of these graves, but it is speculated that it was due to a land shortage. There was a need for a church in this part of town but no land was available—or at least no affordable land.

Is it haunted because a building was constructed on top of these graves? Or may the reason be more sinister? During the early 1900s, a medical school was located near the burying grounds. In those days, medical students often had to procure their own cadavers. It is rumored that many of these students robbed this graveyard. According to legend, many of the corpses dissected in Davidge Hall came from neighboring Westminster. Since medical students have been caught stealing corpses, it isn't hard to believe that some have been successfully stolen and used at the school. In fact, two students were hanged when they were caught red-handed carrying a corpse out of the burying ground.

Some believe one of the spirits that haunts the grounds is one of the students who was hanged for stealing a corpse. The catacombs are allegedly haunted by Frank, who was guilty of stealing several corpses in exchange for money. Medical students who were afraid of getting caught could always find someone desperate enough for money to steal corpses for them.

Over the years, witnesses have reported hearing footsteps, seeing shadowy figures, and smelling strange odors. Sightings have been reported too. Many have sworn to see the spirit of sixteen-year-old Lucia Watson Taylor, kneeling near her grave, as well as Poe sightings.

Some soldiers who were buried here were later dug up and moved to the catacombs. Their spirits may haunt the grounds since their final resting place was disturbed.

In addition to medical students digging up graves, looters have also plundered the graves looking for jewelry or anything else of value that may have been buried along with the deceased.

A woman who was mentally ill and constrained by a straight-jacket for most of her life was buried here. According to some, her restless spirit can still be heard. She had an eerie laugh that reportedly was like a witch's cackle. Even after her death, that laugh has been heard near her grave.

The spirit of a caretaker is said to be one of the spirits here. He roams the graveyard making sure that everything is okay. Some say they have been chased by a shadowy figure with a ghostly shovel when they did something the spirit didn't like, such as showing disrespect to the dead.

Many famous folks have been laid to rest in the Burying Grounds, including Edgar Allan Poe, General Sam Smith, and General James McHenry.

In fact, eighteen generals are buried here, as well as the signer of the Declaration of Independence.

Poe was buried here upon his death but his headstone was replaced with a more elaborate one in 1875 once sufficient funds had been raised for the monument. Poe was found unconscious lying in the street in 1849. He was taken to the hospital where he died a few days later. His cause of death was never discovered.

One of the most famous characters here is not among the dead. He is the Poe Toaster. For many years, a black-clad figure wearing a hat has been spotted bringing flowers and a bottle of cognac to Poe's grave. This mysterious visitor hasn't been since 2009 leaving us to wonder if he has died or was simply tired of making the trek to Poe's grave every January on Poe's birthday.

There hasn't been a burial here since 1943. The congregation disbanded and the church closed in 1977. Maintenance of the building and grounds came under the jurisdiction of the Westminster Preservation Trust Inc. The non-profit group raised close to two million dollars to renovate the building. The Gothic design, magnificent carved oak woodwork, and stained glass windows make it the perfect place for special events. Since 1983, the facility has been a venue for weddings and parties.

Fun Facts about Edgar Allen Poe

Obsessed with cats, Edgar often wrote with a cat atop his shoulder!

He introduced the first recorded literary detective in "The Murders in the Rue Morgue." He is also credited with defining the modern short story.

In his famous poem, "The Raven," Poe originally planned to make it about a parrot rather than a raven. Good thing he changed his mind.

Stull Cemetery

Stull Cemetery

Location: Stull, Kansas

Established: 1867

Visitor Information: Stull is a tiny town about ten miles west of Lawrence, which is in northeast Kansas. Clinton Lake and Clinton State Park are located southeast of Stull. The town can be accessed by US Hwy 40. The cemetery is on the north side of North 1600 Road, just east of East 250 Road. The cemetery is across from the United Methodist Church.

The cemetery is closed to visitors. However, you can easily see inside the chain-link fence. It is not advisable to ignore the "No Trespassing" sign as trespassers have been yelled at and chased away, as well as arrested or fined. Some claim they had shots fired at them. Stull is a tiny community and visitors are quickly noticed. Furthermore, the townspeople are very protective of the old cemetery.

During October, the number of visitors increases significantly. On Halloween night, police position themselves in front of the cemetery to make sure that no one tries to enter the cemetery. On Halloween or any other time, visitors may stay as long as they follow two rules: #1 is to stay outside the fence and #2 is all media and visitors must be gone before midnight. The property owner authorizes authorities to run off anyone that remains after 11:30 p.m.

Stull Road
Stull, Kansas

About the Haunted Cemetery

The stories are so well known that ghost hunters and television and movie producers have filmed here. The popular CW show, *Supernatural*, filmed several scenes of a show from Season Five in the cemetery. In fact, so many have flocked here to explore and confirm the rumors that a local man reportedly destroyed the Stull Evangelical Emmanuel Church in 2002 to discourage visitors. The property owners say that they did not give permission to anyone to do anything to the old church. They were as surprised as the neighbors, who swore they knew nothing until they saw the ruins of the church.

When Stull was established in 1850, no one could have foreseen that its claim to fame would be its cemetery. Originally known as Deer Creek Community, it was settled by six Pennsylvania Dutch families. Nine years later, they established the Evangelical Emmanuel Church. Jacob Hildenbrand donated the parcel of land and by 1867, a lovely stone church and cemetery had been erected.

The town changed its name to Stull in 1899 to honor its first postmaster, Sylvester Stull. For some reason, the town never grew. To this day, there are only a handful of homes and businesses. Despite its size, Stull has managed to garner national recognition.

Its notoriety stems from the legends that grow in popularity year after year. One of these legends is about a young boy who was found dead in his father's field in the early 1900s. According to legend, his father was a farmer who had burned off his field, which is a common farming practice. This ensures the best soil for the next year's crops. Somehow, this child got caught in the fire and was burned to death. The spirit of this boy who died so tragically has been seen ever since that time.

For unknown reasons, a man hanged himself from a tree on the church grounds. A ghostly mist that has been seen by some witnesses is believed to be the spirit of this poor man.

But the scariest story involves Satan. It is said that the Devil himself puts in an appearance in the Stull Cemetery twice a year: on the night of the Spring Equinox and on Halloween. It is believed that the Devil only appears one other place on earth and that is a remote area of India.

You may well wonder why would Satan come to a little cemetery in this sparsely populated hamlet. According to legend, he comes to visit a witch that is buried in this old graveyard. Many believe it is the one marked "Wittich." There used to be a tree that was used for hanging witches on the church grounds. Supposedly, the witch who was hanged and buried in this cemetery was mother of the child of Satan. The baby only lived a few days. Its tiny corpse was buried in Stull Cemetery.

Some witnesses have reported seeing a ghostly boy peering out from behind a tree. Before it was chopped down in 1998 to discourage ghost enthusiasts, many reported seeing shadowy figures dancing around the tree. These were commonly believed to be the spirits of some of these executed witches.

Satan exacts his revenge by taking the souls of those who dare get too close. It is believed that a secret stairway exists and that it is one of the seven portals to Hell. If visitors get too close, they will be pulled down these steps and into Hell.

I know it sounds far-fetched that there is a portal to Hell or that Satan puts in bi-annual appearances, but I do believe this cemetery is haunted. There have been too many paranormal events over the years to ignore or discount. I also have to wonder why the townspeople have gone to such lengths to get rid of visitors. They have destroyed a church, chopped down trees, fired shotguns at visitors, and have pressured police to arrest trespassers. Other places have capitalized on their hauntings with festivals and ghost tours. But these folks have done everything they can to discourage *any* interest. Are they really that protective of a little, old cemetery or is there something more to this story?

FYI: Many nicknames have been assigned to this cemetery over the years, including The Seventh Gate of Hell, Satan's Burial Ground, The Lost Seven Gates of Hell, and Cemetery of the Damned.

Hollywood Cemetery

Hollywood Cemetery

Location: Richmond, Virginia

Established: 1849

Visitor Information: It is open to the public every day from 7:30 a.m.–5:00 p.m. You may explore on your own or take a guided history walking tour Monday to Saturday at 10:00 a.m. and Sundays at 2:00 p.m. from April to November. Segway tours are available by appointment only and trolley tours are offered on Saturdays and Sundays at 1:30 p.m. from April to November.

412 South Cherry Street
Richmond, Virginia 23220

http://www.hollywoodcemetery.org

http://www.nps.gov/nr/travel/richmond/hollywoodcemetery.html

About the Haunted Cemetery

This cemetery is often confused with Hollywood Forever Cemetery, which is located in Hollywood, California. This Virginia cemetery got its name because of the Holly trees that are abundant here.

Overlooking the James River, it is a picturesque cemetery due to these lovely trees and blooming flowers and bushes, as well as the exquisite sculptures and monuments. One particularly fine piece is a ninety-foot granite pyramid that was created to pay tribute to the 18,000 Civil War soldiers buried here (11,000 of which died during the famous Battle of Gettysburg). It dates back to 1869.

Therefore, it should not be surprising that a lot of paranormal activity has been reported near this monument. These reports include two cold spots and moaning.

Also, a little girl and a small dog have been seen many times throughout the years. The girl is believed to be the spirit of Bernadine Rees. She died of fever in 1862 when she was three years old. According to legend, the family dog was loyal and protective of the child. Upon her death, a cast-iron dog sculpture was placed by the girl's grave so that even in death she would never be alone. While this may be true, some accounts say the sculpture was a treasured family heirloom that existed before the child died. It was moved to her grave to save it from being confiscated by the military to melt down and make munitions for the war. Other accounts say this dog statue didn't even belong to the family but was simply put at the child's grave in hopes of saving it from being used to make munitions.

Regardless of how and why it came to be placed at her grave, many have reported the Iron Dog changes direction. They swear that it is pointing one way when they pass it and when they return, it is facing in another direction. Some claim to have been chased by a ghost dog.

The spirits of two other ghost dogs purportedly roam this cemetery. Author Ellen Glasgow is buried here. Her final wish was that her beloved dogs, who were buried in her backyard, be moved to her graveside. Some believe these are the dogs they have seen and heard on occasion near Glasgow's grave.

But the eeriest story associated with this cemetery involves a tunnel and a terrible tragedy. The story takes place in 1925 when the 4,000-foot Church Hill train tunnel collapsed. Approximately 200 workmen were trapped when this happened. Fortunately, there were some survivors. Sadly, others were not so lucky.

One such unfortunate soul was Ben Mosby. The accident left him badly burned and disfigured. Somehow, he dug himself out and limped into the nearby cemetery. Witnesses, realizing he was a survivor in need of help, went after him. They saw him disappear into a mausoleum. They found him inside crumpled up and barely alive. Despite his frightening appearance, they carried him to Grace Hospital where he soon died from his significant injuries. Ever since that time, witnesses have reported seeing a frightening sight that looks more like a monster than a man. They say it has wild eyes, jagged teeth, scars, and a strange gait. Is this the spirit of poor Ben Mosby or someone or something else?

Who or what haunts this place may remain in dispute, but the one indisputable fact is that this cemetery is haunted—and possibly by many lost souls. It's possible that some others that perished in this terrible tunnel tragedy may also haunt the cemetery, perhaps seeking a proper burial so that they can finally rest in peace.

If you visit this cemetery, be sure to look for the life-like cast-iron dog sculpture and the Confederate pyramid monument. Also, you won't want to miss President James Monroe's Tomb. It is an exquisite monument that is on the National Historic Landmark Registry. Another noteworthy monument is President John Tyler's monument. It is located near President James Monroe's monument in the Presidents' Circle. There is also a life-size replica of Confederate President Jefferson Davis. The best view of the scenic James River is from the Presidents' Circle.

FYI: There are roughly 75,000 graves in this 135-acre cemetery and they include some famous folks: President James Monroe, President John Tyler, Clifford Dowdy, Confederate President Jefferson Davis, Author Ellen Glasgow, J.E.B. Stuart, and many Confederate soldiers and officers. In fact, more Confederate generals are buried here than anywhere else in America. Hollywood contains the remains of 28 Confederate generals who died during and after the war.

Hollywood Forever Cemetery

Hollywood Forever Cemetery

Location: Hollywood, California

Established: 1899

Visitor Information: This cemetery is open to the public during the day for self-guided tours. Maps can be purchased, and it might be a good idea to buy one since the cemetery spans sixty acres.

Or you can take a guided tour that promises to be entertaining and informative: www.cemeterytour.com.

There is also a 'Dearly Departed' tour, which lasts three hours aboard a Doomed Buggy. This tour includes other Hollywood sights in addition to the Hollywood cemetery: www.dearlydepartedtours.com.

6000 Santa Monica Blvd.
Hollywood, California 90038

www.hollywoodforever.com

About the Haunted Cemetery

Originally, this cemetery was the Hollywood Memorial Park and extended more than a hundred acres. Forty acres were sold to Paramount Studios in the 1920s. It is said that Paramount is one of the most haunted studios in America because of its proximity to the cemetery. There have been many sightings of spirits wearing vintage clothing in the soundstages. Disembodied voices and footsteps are often heard.

It is commonly believed the spirits are actors and actresses buried in Hollywood Forever Cemetery who have strayed beyond the confines of the cemetery. Perhaps, they are still drawn to the stage and even in the afterlife, they seek applause and attention.

The cemetery fell into a state of disrepair for many years until it was sold in 1998. Major renovations were done, and the cemetery has been restored to its original glory. This is good news given how many people visit it every year. That is partly because it is haunted and also because it is a "who's who" of old Hollywood. Many of the late greats are buried here such as Douglas Fairbanks, Peter Lorre, Alfalfa and Darla Hood (Little Rascals), David White (Bewitched), Bugsy Siegel (legendary mobster), Tyrone Power, Cecil B. DeMille, John Houston, Fay Wray, Nelson Eddy, Marion Davies, Barbara LaMarr, and many more.

There are also monuments that represent actors who are buried elsewhere, such as Jayne Mansfield and Hattie McDaniel.

But the three most notorious residents of

Hollywood Forever Cemetery are its ghosts. Clifton Webb (Mr. Belvedere movies) haunts the Abbey of the Psalms Mausoleum. Paranormal activity includes inexplicable flickering of lights, disembodied voices, cold spots, the smell of cologne, and a specter resembling Clifton Webb—right down to his trademark suit. He sometimes yells or whistles at visitors.

Another spirit who roams the grounds is Virginia Rappe. She was on the cusp of becoming an A-list actress when she died under mysterious circumstances at a Fatty Arbuckle party in 1921. Arbuckle was tried for her murder but was acquitted. Sobbing is often heard near her grave and some have reported suddenly getting very cold when approaching her grave.

The third ghost relates to Rudolph Valentino. Ditra Flame was the daughter of a close friend of

Valentino's. Once when she was hospitalized,
Valentino paid the girl a visit and brought her red roses.
He assured her that she would get well and live many
more years. To further ease her mind, he made her
promise to visit his grave because he was sure he would
die many years before her.

Tragically, Valentino's prediction was more imminent
than he realized. Rudolph Valentino died at age thirty-
one from gastric surgery complications. When
Valentino died, Flame remembered his request and
honored it. She brought red roses to his grave every
year until her death in 1984. She tried to remain
anonymous wearing all black and covered with a veil
but was forced to reveal her identity when so many

"Lady in Black" copycats began coming to the grave and leaving red roses.

The tradition continues with women in black still appearing each year with red roses. Visitors who know about the tradition often bring a red rose and leave it on his crypt during their visit.

Witnesses have seen a veiled woman kneeling at his grave clutching a red rose. When they approach, the figure vanishes but the rose remains. So this begs the question, is this the spirit of the real "Lady in Black" who is still visiting Valentino's grave even in the afterlife?

FYI: Find-a-Grave has compiled a list of burials at Hollywood Forever Cemetery:
http://www.findagrave.com/php/famous.php?page=cem&previousJumpTo=0&previousFameFilter=&FScemeteryid=8033&jumpTo=1&fameLevel=somewhat

And there is an interesting video posted on YouTube detailing a ghost investigation here:
https://www.youtube.com/watch?v=4yJjgYpxzGc

Greenwood Cemetery

Greenwood Cemetery

Location: Decatur, Illinois

Established: Records indicate burials were done here as early as circa 1840, but it was not officially established until 1857.

Visitor Information: This cemetery is open to the public from 8:00 a.m.–4:30 p.m. Check their Facebook page for information about a walking tour option that may soon be available.

You can also see the cemetery and hear stories about it during a Haunted Decatur Tour. These three-hour haunted history and ghost hunting tours depart from the Lincoln Square Theater at 141 N. Main Street: www.haunteddecatur.com.

606 S. Church Street
Decatur, Illinois 62522

https://www.facebook.com/Greenwood-Cemetery-Decatur-Illinois-106976936023491/

About the Haunted Cemetery

There is some evidence to support the theory that this was a Native American burial ground before it became Greenwood Cemetery. Unmarked graves have been found on the south side of the cemetery. It seems that in the early 1800s, settlers began burying their dead in their backyards. This was an era before cemeteries and funeral services. Typically, there were no coffins or embalming procedures. Bodies were wrapped in cloth and buried in a hole that was dug out back of the family home or in close proximity.

Over time, folks began burying their dead in one place and calling it a cemetery or graveyard. In this case, it was Greenwood Cemetery. They didn't realize this was already a sacred burial ground. Native Americans often did not use grave markers so it would have been an easy mistake to make. Even if there had been some indication this was a burial ground, signs or markers had probably been destroyed by the elements. There was also an incident between some early settlers and Native Americans that led to the death of some Native Americans. Their bodies were disposed of quickly in unmarked graves without a proper burial ceremony.

Furthermore, it is believed that Decatur was a stop on the Underground Railroad, which was a collection of safe houses for escaped slaves. Many slaves died on their journey to freedom and some were buried by abolitionists in unmarked graves in Greenwood Cemetery.

The cemetery was the place to bury the dead in this area for many years. That changed when the cemetery fell into a state of disrepair. The situation became even direr when vandals destroyed close to a hundred tombstones in the 1970s. A bad flood in 1903 caused some bodies to be reburied in another section of the cemetery. Some of the caskets were never recovered. They floated away never to be seen again.

All these things could easily explain some of the paranormal activity that has been reported here, but there are documented cases of a lot more ghostly goings-on here than that. One of the most well-known stories is the Greenwood Bride.

This is a tragic tale. A young man and woman fell in love, but the 1920s was a hard time. The country was suffering a depression, and it was a tough time for most folks. They did what they had to in order to survive and take care of their families. This young man became a bootlegger, which was risky but profitable during Prohibition. Her family disapproved of him and forbade her to marry him.

But being young and in love, nothing could stop them. They made a plan to elope, knowing there was nothing their families could do about it once they were married. They were to meet at their favorite spot at midnight after he delivered some illegal liquor to help pay for their trip. She showed up as planned and waited a long time, but he never came. She later learned that he was murdered that night when some greedy men intercepted the bootlegger on his way to his meeting. His body was found the next day along the banks of the Sangamon River.

The bride never recovered from the loss of her beloved. She went mad with grief. After crying and screaming for hours, her mother finally got her to go to bed. When they went into her room to check on her the next day, they discovered she had snuck out. Her body was found near the same spot where her finance had been discovered. It seems that she had no desire to live without him.

She was buried in her wedding dress that her parents found among her things when looking for a burial dress. They thought it was fitting to bury her in it and so they did. She was laid to rest in Greenwood Cemetery. Ever since that time, witnesses have seen a figure wearing what looks like a wedding dress walking around the cemetery. She appears to be crying. Many believe this is the spirit of the bride who lost her true love on the eve of their wedding.

She should not be mistaken with a lady in a long white dress who is sometimes seen during the day around the Barrackman family burial plot. There are four stone steps that extend up a little hill to their four graves. This ghostly lady is seen sitting on the steps weeping softly. If you approach her or when the sun sets, she will disappear. Is she perhaps a member of the Barrackman family?

Some folks have seen what they thought were funerals in progress but when the attendees vanish right in front of their eyes, they realize they are seeing a phantom funeral.

Another eerie occurrence is the Greenwood Ghost Lights. These have been seen on the south end of the cemetery. They have been described as little round balls of light that mysteriously appear and disappear.

They have become known as ghost lights because there is no logical reason for their appearance or disappearance. You can see for yourself. While you cannot enter the cemetery at night, you can still see the lights if conditions are right and you are in the right place. Park your vehicle in the gravel parking lot across from the cemetery, just outside the fence. Watch the hills closely and you may be rewarded with ghost lights.

There is another haunted area where a beautiful mausoleum used to be before the flood when Mother Nature did such damage that it had to be razed in the mid-1960s. People have reported hearing screaming, whispering, and crying where it once stood. Ghost hunters have documented paranormal activity here, including cold spots and EVPs.

Another area of the cemetery that has seen its fair share of paranormal activity is the southwest end. This is where some Civil War soldiers were laid to rest. But they don't seem to be doing much resting.

Perhaps they are unable to rest since many are in "Unknown Soldier" graves. Or perhaps they just have a hard time accepting their premature deaths. Whatever the reason, the spirits of these deceased soldiers have been heard through cries of despair and footsteps that sound like boots marching. They have been known to touch or push visitors on occasion.

One time when a young man was exploring the cemetery, he was approached by a man no older than nineteen or twenty years old. He was dressed in an old gray coat and asked for help getting home before vanishing right before the visitor's eyes.

Chestnut Hill Cemetery

Chestnut Hill Cemetery

Location: Exeter, Rhode Island

Established: Circa 1838

Visitor Information:

Ten Rod Road/Victory Highway
Exeter, Rhode Island 02822

Take I-95 to Victory Highway and follow this road for roughly five miles until you see a small white church on the left. The cemetery is behind Chestnut Hill Baptist Church.

Mercy's grave is in the center of the cemetery, which is open to visitors. The church was added to the National Register of Historic Places in 1978.

About the Haunted Cemetery

Lots of cemeteries share similar stories about a woman in white or disembodied voices, but finally at Chestnut Hill Cemetery, we have something a tad different—a graveyard vampire.

The story begins in the 1800s. There was a tuberculosis (TB) epidemic across North America and Europe during the 1800s. Documentation shows that 70 to 90 percent of the population of North America and Europe contracted the disease. With less than 20 percent survival rate, there was a well-deserved hysteria and fear associated with this disease.

Also known as consumption, phthisis, and white plague, TB was a painful affliction. Patients suffered a long time with bad bouts of coughing that often included coughing up blood, difficulty breathing, chills, weight loss due to loss of appetite, fever, chest pain, pale or translucent skin, and fatigue.

There was no cure, and it was highly contagious. Across America and Europe, sanitariums sprang up to accommodate all those who had been stricken with it. While there was no cure, there were treatments believed to ease the suffering including sitting outside in the cold air for hours and lung machines.

As often happened, once one or two family members contracted TB, the rest soon followed. The Brown family of Exeter, Rhode Island were among those odds. Mary Brown (mother) and one of her three children were the first to be diagnosed with consumption. They soon succumbed to death. Next, the two remaining children, Mercy and Edwin, were struck. Reportedly, Mercy used to sit on Edwin's chest late at night. Later on, when folks learned of this, they believed that Mercy had been trying to claim Edwin's body. They thought this supported the rumor that Mercy was not normal. In all likelihood, this was probably a figment of Edwin's delirious, feverish mind.

Before she was struck ill, Mercy was often seen playing in the graveyard. She was seen talking to herself and "dancing" between the tombstones. The community thought her behavior was very odd.

Fear spread like fire through towns as more and more lives were lost. People grabbed onto any hope or tactic to save loved ones. Exeter was no exception. Because of their crazy fear and rumors based on Mercy's behavior and appearance before her death, folks got it into their heads that Mercy Brown was a vampire and a curse on their community. Never mind that many other TB patients "spewed blood," had deathly pale or translucent skin, and "vacant eyes."

Mercy Lena Brown died in 1892 at the age of nineteen. She was buried in a quiet ceremony in the church graveyard. But not for long. All this talk of vampires and curses led the community to action. Something had to be done to stop this curse, and they thought they had the answer. They exhumed her body, which was still intact. In fact, she bled when poked and prodded. That really scared the townspeople, who thought she should be more decayed, more corpse-like, even though she had only recently been buried.

Someone suggested her heart had to be removed to end the madness. And they did. Her chest was cut open and her heart was cut out. What they did next was even more inconceivable if that's possible. They placed her heart on a large stone and set fire to it. Afterward, they collected the ashes and added water and herbs to concoct an elixir. George Brown served it to Edwin Brown in the hopes of saving his dying son. Without so much as a word or gesture, they threw the mutilated body of Mercy Brown back into her grave, confident this would be the end of their troubles.

Quite the contrary, Edwin Brown soon died of consumption, and it remained a deadly epidemic for many more years. All that was achieved by removing Mercy's heart was disturbing her final resting place, and we all know that is bad news. This is when supernatural activity began at Chestnut Hill Cemetery. Mysterious blue lights have been seen ever since. A shadowy figure wearing dark clothing, like a mourning dress, has been seen roaming around the cemetery. She moves between the same tombstones and in the same way Mercy was said to have done when she used to play in the cemetery. Mercy's frequent visits to the cemetery may have been nothing more than a child taking comfort in visiting her mother and sister's graves.

She has been known to push people who are visiting loved ones. Is she trying to play or simply mad about what was done to her? If you visit this cemetery, maybe you will get a chance to ask her for yourself. Her grave can be found in the center of the cemetery as part of the Brown plot. You will notice that her gravestone is firmly anchored to prevent theft.

FYI: *What is a vampire?*

A vampire is "undead"; the dead brought back to life. They must drink the blood of the living to retain their immortality. There are only five ways to kill a vampire:

*direct sunlight

*wooden stake through the heart

*solid silver handcuffs (this must be combined with another method, such as leaving the body in direct sunlight)

*big fire that must burn at least thirty minutes to one hour

*chop off head using solid silver knife

Nevertheless, the best way to get rid of a vampire—if you believe in them—is to stop it before it becomes immortal. This is done by digging up the grave of the suspected vampire and performing a ceremony that involves removing the heart. Believe it or not, this ritual is still performed in rural areas of southeastern Europe. There was a case in Romania in 2015 when six men were prosecuted for this very crime: http://www.abovetopsecret.com/forum/thread11623 7/pg1.

This is not a hoax. I first learned about this story on Travel Channel when Josh Gates of *Expedition Unknown* interviewed the prosecutor and saw the crime photos. I also found more instances of similar activity by doing an Internet search.

It seems that Mercy Brown was a victim of an age-old tradition. Scary stuff! If you can get past the

jerky camera movement, this is a good video tour of the cemetery and discussion of this legend.
https://www.youtube.com/watch?v=NhkJErqcu-k

El Campo Santo Cemetery

El Campo Santo Cemetery

Location: San Diego, California

Established: 1849

Visitor Information:

El Campo Santo Cemetery is open to the public. It is also a State Historical Landmark.

2410 San Diego Avenue (part of Old Town San Diego Historical Park)
San Diego, California 92110

http://www.yelp.com/biz/el-campo-santo-cemetery-san-diego

There are some ghost tours that include the cemetery and Whaley House:

http://www.ghostsandgravestones.com/san-diego/

http://www.oldtownsmosthaunted.com/

http://www.trolleytours.com/san-diego/ghost-tours.asp

About the Haunted Cemetery

El Campo Santo means "sacred ground." This Catholic
cemetery is the second oldest cemetery in San Diego.
There have been no burials in this 477-grave cemetery
since 1880. Once upon a time, this cemetery was much
larger, extending all the way to Old Town Avenue, but
as land became a premium in San Diego, acres were
sold off and graves were moved—or not.

According to some sources, roads and buildings
have literally been built on top of graves. It began in the
1800s when a street was built through the cemetery so
that a horse-drawn street car could go right through
town. This meant covering up more than a dozen
graves. When this street was later paved and named San

Diego Boulevard, it was wider than the original road. This meant it covered up another half dozen or so graves. We know that at least eighteen graves were concealed due to roadwork but some accounts put it as high as thirty graves.

Some of the most haunted places in the world are those where graves have been disturbed. When you disturb a grave, you are disturbing the dead, which is never a good idea. As a result, a lot of supernatural activity has been reported.

Area homes and businesses have complained of power bumps, power outages, and appliances and alarms tripping off and on for no logical reason. The power company is always mystified when these incidents are reported as the events are confined to the immediate area around the cemetery and do not coincide with any malfunctions or outages.

Another sign of supernatural activity is cold spots. These are small, defined places that are unseasonably and unreasonably cold. Cold spots have been reported by lots of different people in the same areas of the cemetery.

Be careful where you park as car trouble is often reported by those who park in front of the graveyard. They return to find their car battery dead. Some have run back to their vehicles upon hearing their car alarms but find no one or nothing near their vehicle.

A psychic named Virginia Marco has reported some children spirits, including one little boy she helped cross over and a gravedigger entity.

But the biggest telltale sign of paranormal

activity is the sightings that have been reported. Native American and Hispanic spirits have been seen in the evenings seemingly floating just above the ground.

A torso has been seen that is believed by many to by Yankee Jim, who is buried here. Specters wearing Victorian costumes and park employee uniforms have been seen. As people approached them to ask a question, they were shocked when these figures vanished into thin air.

FYI: While in San Diego, be sure to visit nearby Whaley House. Not only is it one of the most haunted houses in America, it is one of only two houses that have been officially certified as "haunted" by the US government. Yankee Jim is the resident ghost. It is believed he also haunts the cemetery where he was buried after being hanged. Here is a link to the investigation done by Travel Channel's *Ghost Adventures*:
https://www.youtube.com/watch?v=1lF9ls4HI
2Y.

Fun Facts about Whaley House

*It has served as a theater, reception hall, courtroom, recital hall, and private residence.

*It cost $10,000 to build in the mid-1800s.

*It took Thomas Whaley 204 days to travel from New York to California. When he arrived in San Francisco, there were already 150 vessels in port. They were full of men like him who had come out West to seek their fortune.

Gravesite of Yankee Jim

Howard Street Cemetery

Howard Street Cemetery

Location: Salem, Massachusetts

Established: Circa 1801

Visitor Information: The cemetery is open to the public during daylight hours. Trespassing after hours may result in arrest and prosecution. The cemetery is beside the Old Salem Jail. You can explore on your own or take a tour:

Salem Historical Tours, www.salemhistoricaltours.com

Spellbound Tours Witchcraft & Cemetery Tour, www.spellboundtours.com

Salem Night Tours, www.salemghosttours.com

29 Howard Street
Salem, Massachusetts 01970

https://www.facebook.com/pages/Friends-of-the-Howard-Street-Cemetery-Salem-MA/195539430469460

While in Salem, be sure to visit Old Burying Ground. It is the oldest cemetery in the city and the second oldest in America, dating back to 1637. Some of its "residents" include former Massachusetts Governor Samuel Bradstreet, Jonathan Corwin and John Hawthorne (Salem Witch Trial judges), and Richard Moore (pilgrim).

About the Haunted Cemetery

This is the third oldest cemetery in Salem. Many distinguished folks have been buried here, such as Artist George Ropes Jr., whose works can be seen in the National Gallery of Art and Peabody Essex Museum. There are Revolutionary War soldiers buried here, including Colonel Sam Carlton, who was at Valley Forge with George Washington. Relatives of author Nathaniel Hawthorne are laid to rest here, as well as numerous sea captains.

But the most famous person buried among Howard Street Cemetery's three hundred graves is Giles Corey. This story begins in 1659 when Corey moved to Salem after marrying his first wife, Margaret.

She died in 1684, and he married Martha in 1690. A short time later, rumors began circulating that Martha was a witch. On Monday, March 21, 1692 she was arrested for witchcraft.

During her trial, Giles testified against his wife. He told the court how his ox and cat suffered mysterious illnesses that led to their deaths. He also told the court that he often caught her up late at night kneeling in front of the fire as if in a trance. As you can tell, real evidence was not needed during these witch trials.

Ironically, Giles Corey was arrested three days after his testimony on the very same charges. Five women came forward claiming he had practiced witchcraft against them. Talk about karma.

During the proceedings, the five afflicted women had seizures while appearing in court. The judge was convinced Corey was practicing witchcraft on them and ordered that his hands be tied so that he would not be able to do witchcraft.

To the frustration of the sheriff and judge, Corey would not enter a plea. Because of this, Corey was tortured by the sheriff. According to law at that time, if a person refused to enter a plea, one could be coerced out of him using any means necessary.

Sheriff Corwin practiced the traditional torture, which was to strip the prisoner of his clothes, lay him on the ground, and place a board laden down with heavy stones atop of it. But it didn't stop there. As each day passed and the prisoner still hadn't given in, more stones were added to the board. After several days of this horrific torture, Corey died.

According to legend, Giles Corey placed a curse on the sheriff and the town of Salem for his mistreatment. Just before he died, he yelled, "Damn you! I curse you and Salem!"

At thirty years old, Sheriff Corwin suffered a massive heart attack that killed him just a couple of years later. Coincidence or curse?

Many other sheriffs suffered strange fates like rare blood disorders and an abnormally high number of painful heart attacks described as feeling like something was sitting on their chest. This kept occurring until the 1970s when the prison was moved to another location. Prior to that time, some sheriffs have reported awakening during the night and seeing an apparition in their bedroom or feeling an unseen presence on their chest. The curse may be gone but not Giles Corey. His ghost has been seen in Howard Street Cemetery before and after any town tragedy. For example, his spirit was seen just before the Great Salem Fire of 1914.

You can see Giles Corey's marker at the Salem Witch Trials Memorial Park (see below) on Liberty Street.

FYI: The Salem Witch Trials were actually a series of hearings that took place in Essex, Middlesex, and Suffolk counties. They took place between February 1692 and May 1693. More than 150 were arrested and some died in prison before their court date. The court convicted 29 people of witchcraft, which was a felony. All were hanged at Gallows Hill. Today, you can visit Gallows Hill, but while some question whether this was the real Gallows Hill, most believe it is. You can also visit many other haunted sites,

including the House of Seven Gables, Ropes Mansion, Custom House, Town Hall, Joshua Ward House, Hawthorne Hotel, and Baker's Island.

For more information and tour options:

http://www.hauntedsalem.com/guidehaunted.html

http://www.tripadvisor.com/Tourism-g60954-Salem_Massachusetts-Vacations.html

http://www.salem.org/

The building in the background is the Old Salem Jail

Union Cemetery

Union Cemetery

Location: Easton, Connecticut

Established: Burials date back to 1700s, but the cemetery wasn't officially established until circa 1840s.

Visitor Information: The cemetery is open to the public during daylight hours. Please be respectful as funerals and burials still occur here. The cemetery is beside Easton Baptist Church, which is at 29 Church Road.

Church Road (Off Stepney Road at the junction of Route 59 & 136)
Eason, Connecticut 06612

https://www.facebook.com/pages/Union-Cemetery-Easton-Connecticut/137966326225734

About the Haunted Cemetery

Some say this is the most haunted cemetery in America. It has been investigated by lots of ghost groups over the years, including the New England Society for Psychic Resources and renowned paranormal researchers and demonologists Ed & Lorraine Warren.

The most notorious spirit is the White Lady. She has been seen by many credible witnesses, such as police officers, firefighters, and Ed Warren. He has even caught her on camera. His photos can be seen in his book, *Graveyard* (see below).

If you see a glowing specter with long, dark hair wearing a white bonnet and long white dress or nightgown, that would be the White Lady.

Your best chance of seeing her is in the cemetery drifting or floating among the graves or sobbing softly. She also puts in an appearance on Route 59. Some vehicles slam on brakes to avoid hitting her but most are not able to stop in time. They brace for the hit but pass through her—a sure clue you are encountering a spirit.

One time, however, a fireman was on his way home from work in 1993 when he saw a woman on the road. He was nearly blinded by her bright appearance. He slammed on the brakes and watched as his car went right through the woman. Badly shaken and unsure about what had just happened, he pulled the truck over and got out to check on the victim. She had vanished. But sure enough, there was a small dent in his vehicle where he had hit her. This is the only time, relating to the White Lady, that physical evidence has corroborated a spiritual manifestation.

The White Lady also reportedly haunts Stepney Cemetery in nearby Monroe. But who is she? One legend has it she was a woman who was murdered in the early 1900s and her body hidden in a sinkhole behind a church. Another legend says she died during childbirth and is still searching for her lost child.

Even if you don't see the White Lady during your visit, you may catch a glimpse of Red Eyes. Many people have reported seeing sinister-looking red eyes peering out of the bushes as they walk past the cemetery. Some believe this is the spirit of Earle Kellog, a man who was burned to death in 1935 across the street from the cemetery.

There have been a few accounts of a ghostly hobo. He walks the fence along the cemetery's perimeter. There have even been reports of ghostly soldiers, a baby crying, footsteps, animal sounds, and rocks thrown by an unseen presence.

FYI: Ed and Lorraine Warren are not only credible experts on paranormal and demonology, but are renowned. Among their most famous cases was the Amityville haunting. They have written several intriguing books including *The Demonologist* and

Graveyard, **which is all about their paranormal encounters at Union Cemetery. Ed Warren is buried in Stepney Cemetery. For more about them, visit**

https://en.wikipedia.org/wiki/Ed_and_Lorraine_Wa
rren **and**
https://www.youtube.com/watch?v=GNYSYWhYydY

&list=PL3te6uBOifb6_aKBzeBiqMiDD2lWQ9eQy.

More Haunted Cemeteries worth Mentioning

Boot Hill Cemetery (formerly Tombstone Cemetery)

Boot Hill Cemetery (Arizona) has more outlaws, prospectors, and gunslingers buried here than anywhere else in America. The list includes Wild Bill Hickok, Billy Clanton, Frank and Tom McLaury, Calamity Jane, and Seth Bullock. Ghostly figures have been seen wearing cowboy hats and gun holders. They appear to be floating or rising up out of the ground, and they disappear when anyone approaches to see what's going on.

Key West Cemetery, Key West (FL)

Key West Cemetery (Florida) is located in Key West's historic Old Town. As many as 100,000 people are buried here, which is more than the current population. It is haunted by a Bahamian woman, who appears when anyone is goofing around or showing disrespect to the dead.

Mt. Carmel Cemetery (Illinois) is reportedly haunted by Al Capone, who is buried here. There is also a ghost named Julia.

Oakdale Cemetery (North Carolina) is haunted by the spirits of Civil War soldiers and by Rose O'Neal "Rebel Rose" Greenhow. She was a Confederate spy. Her story is both remarkable and tragic. Perhaps that is why her ghost is still seen here. But no death is more tragic than that of Captain Martin's daughter, who died at sea. Her body was preserved in a rum barrel until she returned home and had a proper burial at Oakdale Cemetery. She has been seen and heard playing among the tombstones.

Oakdale Cemetery, Wilmington (NC)

Robinson Woods Indian Burial Grounds (Illinois) is a Native American Burial Ground with many missing tombstones. Indians did not use grave markers so many have been dug up by mistake. This disturbance of the dead has led to all kinds of paranormal activity, including the sound of drums playing, mysterious lights, disembodied voices, and shadowy figures. Some speculate if some of this activity doesn't come from

Potawatomi Chief Alexander Robinson, who was buried here in 1872. There is a simple tombstone marking his grave.

Unitarian Churchyard (South Carolina) is haunted by the ghost of Annabel Lee, who used to meet her lover in this graveyard. Her father ended the relationship and a heartbroken Annabel died of yellow fever a few months later. Annabel was buried in the same cemetery where she spent so many happy hours with her beloved. It is believed that her spirit is searching for him to this day.

Cemetery Trivia

A **cemetery** or **graveyard** is a place where the remains of deceased people are buried or interred. The word *cemetery* from the Greek word κοιμητήριον, meaning "sleeping place" indicates the land is specifically designated as a burial ground. The word "graveyard" was not used until the early nineteenth century.

A person's remains can be placed in a coffin, tomb, sarcophagus, mausoleum, columbarium, or something similar. This is usually preceded by a funeral service.

Visitors often bring items when visiting graves, such as flowers. Roses are the most common but any cut flowers can be left except on Jewish graves. Visitors to Jewish cemeteries often leave a small stone on top of the tombstone rather than flowers. The idea is that flowers will soon wilt and die but a stone lasts forever. Small wooden crosses or a Star of David are sometimes left on graves. Other popular items are funeral wreaths and candles.

Once upon a time, family cemeteries were common. Settlers used a small area of their land as a family plot. Sometimes, it extended to friends or the entire community. Today, private cemeteries are rare. Burials in public cemeteries are more common, although wealthy folks with lots of land still opt for private family cemeteries that include beloved pets.

Boot Hill Cemetery has more Old West gunslingers, miners, and outlaws than any other cemetery in America. One of the most well-known tombstones reads, "Here Lies Lester Moore 4 slugs from a 44 no less no more."

Arlington National Cemetery (pictured here) is a 624-acre national military cemetery in Arlington, Virginia.

The biggest number of Civil War interments in America is at **Vicksburg National Cemetery**.

The **oldest pet cemetery** is in Green Country, Illinois. It was discovered by Archaeologist Stewart Schrever, who believes it dates back to 6500 BC. The oldest operating pet cemetery in America is Hartsdate Pet Cemetery in New York, established in 1896.

The only cemetery in the US that faces north-south is in Rayne, Louisiana. **Saint Joseph's Cemetery** is listed in *Ripley's Believe It or Not!*

The **five most beautiful cemeteries** in the world include Highgate Cemetery (London), St. Louis Cemetery #1 (New Orleans), Central Cemetery (Vienna), Bonaventure (Savannah), and Novodevichy Cemetery (Moscow).

The **oldest cemetery** in the United States is Grove Street Cemetery (Connecticut). Some graves date back to the mid-1700s, but it was officially established in 1797.

FYI: Ancient Egyptians believed the body would be needed in their next life so they preserved or mummified it. Organs were removed (and saved in airtight jars) and then the body was dried out using salt. The body was then wrapped up tight in cloth. It was then stored in a sarcophagus until it was "reclaimed" in the next life.

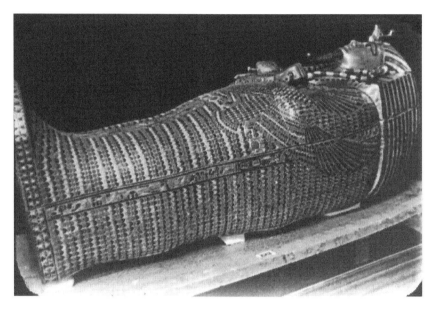

Pictured here is the ornate gold coffin of the Egyptian King Tut. It was one of three coffins safeguarded inside an enormous stone sarcophagus. King Tut ascended to the throne at the age of nine, ruling less than ten years before his death.

Dear Reader,

Thank you for buying or borrowing **Spookiest Cemeteries**. I hope you enjoyed it—and learned a lot.

I spent a great deal of time compiling this information into what I believe is an easy-to-read, useful reference. I would love to hear from you if you'd like to post a comment on www.terrancezepke.com. I do respond to all comments. If you'd like to learn more about hauntings and receive a FREE "Fifty Fun Facts About Ghosts" report, be sure to sign up for my *Mostly Ghostly* blog.

I would also like to ask you to please share your feedback about this book on Amazon or Goodreads so that other readers might discover this title too.

Authors appreciate readers more than you realize, and we dearly love and depend upon good reviews. If you've never posted a review before, it is easy to do…just tell folks what you liked or didn't like about this book and why you (hopefully) recommend it: http://www.amazon.com/Terrance-Zepke/e/B000APJNIA/.

Thank you again for your interest in this book. If you enjoyed it, you may want to check out more books in this series, including *Spookiest Lighthouses* and *Spookiest Battlefields*.

Terrance

TERRANCE ZEPKE

Series Reading Order

& Guide

Series List

Most Haunted Series

Terrance Talks Travel Series

Spookiest Series

Stop Talking Series

Carolinas for Kids Series

Ghosts of the Carolinas Series

Books & Guides for the Carolinas Series

& Other Books by Terrance Zepke

Terrance Zepke

Introduction

Here is a list of titles by Terrance Zepke. They are presented in chronological order although they do not need to be read in any particular order.

Also included is an author bio, a personal message from Terrance, and some other information you may find helpful.

All books are available as eBooks and print books. They can be found on Amazon, Barnes and Noble, Kobo, Apple iBooks, Smashwords, or through your favorite independent bookseller.

For more about this author and her books visit her Author Page at http://www.amazon.com/Terrance-Zepke/e/B000APJNIA/.

You can also connect with Terrance on Twitter @terrancezepke or on

www.facebook.com/terrancezepke

www.pinterest.com/terrancezepke

www.goodreads.com/terrancezepke

151

Sign up for weekly email notifications of the *Terrance Talks Travel* blog to be the first to learn about new episodes of her travel show, travel tips, free downloadable TRAVEL REPORTS, and discover her TRIP PICK OF THE WEEK at www.terrancetalkstravel.com or sign up for her *Mostly Ghostly* blog at www.terrancezepke.com.

You can follow her travel show, **TERRANCE TALKS TRAVEL: ÜBER ADVENTURES on** www.blogtalkradio.com/terrancetalkstravel or subscribe to it at **iTunes.**

≈

Terrance Zepke is co-host of the writing show, **A WRITER'S JOURNEY: FROM BLANK PAGE TO PUBLISHED.** All episodes can be found on **iTunes** or on www.terrancezepke.com.

AUTHOR BIO

Terrance Zepke studied Journalism at the University of Tennessee and later received a Master's degree in Mass Communications from the University of South Carolina. She studied parapsychology at the renowned Rhine Research Center.

Zepke spends much of her time happily traveling around the world but always returns home to the Carolinas where she lives part-time in both states. She has written hundreds of articles and close to three dozen books. She is the host of *Terrance Talks Travel: Über Adventures* and co-host of *A Writer's Journey: From Blank Page to Published*. Additionally, this award-winning and best-selling author has been featured in many publications and programs, such as NPR, CNN, The Washington Post, Associated Press, Travel with Rick Steves, Around the World, Publishers Weekly, World Travel & Dining with Pierre Wolfe, Good Morning Show, The Learning Channel, and The Travel Channel.

When she's not investigating haunted places, searching for pirate treasure, or climbing lighthouses, she is most likely packing for her next adventure to some far flung place, such as Reykjavik or Kwazulu Natal. Some of her favorite adventures include piranha fishing on the

Amazon, shark cage diving in South Africa, hiking the Andes Mountains Inca Trail, camping in the Himalayas, and dog-sledding in the Arctic Circle.

According to Zepke, her favorite haunted place is the Stanley Hotel and the creepiest overnight ghost investigation she ever did was the Trans-Allegheny Lunatic Asylum. Her favorite island in the U.S. is Kiawah (SC) and outside of the U.S. it is Madagascar (Africa), favorite city in the U.S. is Charleston (SC) and her favorite international city is London (England), and her favorite adventure destination is Africa, especially southern and East Africa. While she will rough it for a good adventure, Zepke enjoys five-star cruises, first class, and champagne.

MOST HAUNTED SERIES

A Ghost Hunter's Guide to the Most Haunted Places in America (2012)
https://read.amazon.com/kp/embed?asin=B00 85SG22O&preview=newtab&linkCode=kpe&ref =cm_sw_r_kb_dp_zerQwb1AMJoR4

A Ghost Hunter's Guide to the Most Haunted Houses in America (2013)
https://read.amazon.com/kp/embed?asin=B00 C3PUMGC&preview=newtab&linkCode=kpe&re f_=cm_sw_r_kb_dp_BfrQwb1WF1Y6T

A Ghost Hunter's Guide to the Most Haunted Hotels & Inns in America (2014)
https://read.amazon.com/kp/embed?asin=B00 C3PUMGC&preview=newtab&linkCode=kpe

≈

TERRANCE TALKS TRAVEL SERIES

Terrance Talks Travel: A Pocket Guide to South Africa (2015)
https://read.amazon.com/kp/embed?asin=B00 PSTFTLI&preview=newtab&linkCode=kpe&ref _=cm_sw_r_kb_dp_pirQwb12XZX65

Terrance Talks Travel: A Pocket Guide to African Safaris (2015)
https://read.amazon.com/kp/embed?asin=B00 PSTFZSA&preview=newtab&linkCode=kpe&ref _=cm_sw_r_kb_dp_jhrQwb0P8Z87G

Terrance Talks Travel: A Pocket Guide to Adventure Travel (2015)
https://read.amazon.com/kp/embed?asin=B00 UKMAVQG&preview=newtab&linkCode=kpe&re f_=cm_sw_r_kb_dp_ThrQwb1PVVZAZ

Terrance Talks Travel: A Pocket Guide to Florida Keys (including Key West & The Everglades) (2016)
http://www.amazon.com/Terrance-Zepke/e/B00OAPJNIA/ref=sr_ntt_srch_lnk_1?qi d=1457641303&sr=8-1

SPOOKIEST SERIES

Spookiest Lighthouses (2013)
https://read.amazon.com/kp/embed?asin=B00EAAQA2S&preview

Spookiest Battlefields (2015)
https://read.amazon.com/kp/embed?asin=B00XUSWS3G&preview=newtab&linkCode=kpe&ref_=cm_sw_r_kb_dp_okrQwb0TR9F8M

Spookiest Cemeteries (2016)
http://www.amazon.com/Terrance-Zepke/e/B000APJNIA/ref=sr_ntt_srch_lnk_1?qid=1457641303&sr=8-1

STOP TALKING SERIES

Stop Talking & Start Writing Your Book (2015)
https://read.amazon.com/kp/embed?asin=B01
2YHTIAY&preview=newtab&linkCode=kpe&ref
=cm_sw_r_kb_dp_qlrQwb1N7G3YF

Stop Talking & Start Publishing Your Book
(2015)
https://read.amazon.com/kp/embed?asin=B01
3HHV1LE&preview=newtab&linkCode=kpe&ref
=cm_sw_r_kb_dp_WlrQwb1F63MFD

Stop Talking & Start Selling Your Book (2015)
https://read.amazon.com/kp/embed?asin=B01
5YAO33K&preview=newtab&linkCode=kpe&ref
=cm_sw_r_kb_dp_ZkrQwb188J8BE

≈

CAROLINAS FOR KIDS SERIES

Lighthouses of the Carolinas for Kids (2009)
http://www.amazon.com/Lighthouses-
Carolinas-Kids-Terrance-
Zepke/dp/1561644293/ref=asap_bc?ie=UTF8

Pirates of the Carolinas for Kids (2009)
https://read.amazon.com/kp/embed?asin=B01
BJ3VSWK&preview=newtab&linkCode=kpe&ref
_=cm_sw_r_kb_dp_rGrXwboXDTSTA

Ghosts of the Carolinas for Kids (2011)
https://read.amazon.com/kp/embed?asin=B01
BJ3VSVQ&preview=newtab&linkCode=kpe&ref_
=cm_sw_r_kb_dp_XLrXwboE7N1AK

≈

GHOSTS OF THE CAROLINAS SERIES

Ghosts of the Carolina Coasts (1999)
http://www.amazon.com/Ghosts-Carolina-Coasts-Terrance-Zepke/dp/1561641758/ref=asap_bc?ie=UTF8

The Best Ghost Tales of South Carolina (2004)
http://www.amazon.com/Best-Ghost-Tales-South-Carolina/dp/1561643068/ref=asap_bc?ie=UTF8

Ghosts & Legends of the Carolina Coasts (2005)
https://read.amazon.com/kp/embed?asin=B01AGQJABW&preview=newtab&linkCode=kpe&ref_=cm_sw_r_kb_dp_VKrXwb1Q09794

The Best Ghost Tales of North Carolina (2006)
https://read.amazon.com/kp/embed?asin=B01BJ3VSV6&preview=newtab&linkCode=kpe&ref_=cm_sw_r_kb_dp_6IrXwb0XKT90Q

BOOKS & GUIDES FOR THE CAROLINAS SERIES

Pirates of the Carolinas (2005)

http://www.amazon.com/Pirates-Carolinas-Terrance-Zepke/dp/1561643440/ref=asap_bc?ie=UTF8

Coastal South Carolina: Welcome to the Lowcountry (2006)

http://www.amazon.com/Coastal-South-Carolina-Welcome-Lowcountry/dp/1561643483/ref=asap_bc?ie=UTF8

Coastal North Carolina: Its Enchanting Islands, Towns & Communities (2011)

http://www.amazon.com/Coastal-North-Carolina-Terrance-Zepke/dp/1561645117/ref=asap_bc?ie=UTF8

Lighthouses of the Carolinas: A Short History & Guide (2011)

https://read.amazon.com/kp/embed?asin=B01AGQJA7G&preview=newtab&linkCode=kpe&ref_=cm_sw_r_k b_dp_UHrXwb09A22P1

MORE BOOKS BY TERRANCE ZEPKE

Lowcountry Voodoo: Tales, Spells & Boo Hags (2009)
https://read.amazon.com/kp/embed?asin=B01 8WAGUC6&preview=newtab&linkCode=kpe&re f_=cm_sw_r_kb_dp_UmrQwb19AVSYG

The Encyclopedia of Cheap Travel: Save Up to 90% on Lodging, Flights, Tours, Cruises & More! (2011)
https://read.amazon.com/kp/embed?asin=B00 5WKGNKY&preview=newtab&linkCode=kpe&re f_=cm_sw_r_kb_dp_InrQwb18QTWGS

Ghosts of Savannah (2012)
http://www.amazon.com/Ghosts-Savannah-Terrance-Zepke/dp/1561645303/ref=asap_bc?ie=UTF8

*Fiction books written under a pseudonym

≈

Message from the Author

Since I have written so many books I often get asked for writing advice. My answer is simple. Write about what you are passionate about. Don't try to cash in on the latest trend or most lucrative genre. Stick to what you know and love. This will shine through in your writing, which will ultimately lead to a successful and happy career.

If you're like me and you have a lot of interests, then by all means feel free to write in more than one genre. If you are considering pursuing writing trans-genre be aware that you will have to work a lot harder to appeal to different audiences. I have created and maintain two different websites, write two blogs, and host two different podcasts due to my diverse audience. On www.terrancezepke.com I have created **Ghost Town** and **Hints for Halloween**, showcase my paranormal book series, and feature my *Mostly Ghostly* blog. On www.terrancetalkstravel.com the content is all about travel, including my travel books, *Terrance Talks Travel* blog, TRIP PICKS, travel reports, and **Über Adventures Show**.

This brings me to another popular question. What is my favorite book? This is going to sound like a cop out but they all are near and dear to me. Seriously! My publisher does not assign me book projects. I choose my own projects, so it is something I am knowledgeable and passionate about or I wouldn't have chosen to do it. I really enjoy researching and writing the ghost books. What's not to like? I get to poke around in creepy cemeteries, spooky lighthouses, old asylums, and haunted houses searching for restless spirits—and on occasion I have found them too! I get to research the history of these places and being a huge history buff that is exciting as the investigations.

I am enthusiastic about my travel titles. I love talking about travel and sharing ways to travel cheaper and better and to reveal little known destinations and experiences. I am so proud and excited about my TERRANCE TALKS TRAVEL book series. The first book, *Terrance Talks Travel: A Pocket Guide to South Africa*, soon became an Amazon #1 bestseller and it remains one of my best-selling books. That is thrilling for me as it shows me that I have done my job conveying not only my knowledge, but also my passion for South Africa to my readers.

But every book holds a special place in my heart. *Lighthouses of the Carolinas* was the first book I ever wrote so that makes is near and dear to me, especially since the second edition came out recently. I still remember how crazy excited I was signing that first publishing contract! *Ghosts of the Carolina Coasts* is the first ghost book I ever wrote and quickly became the #1 selling regional ghost book. That success helped pave the way for other ghost books, so I will always have a special fondness for it. All these books have helped me connect with readers who share my passion for the paranormal and for travel. *The world is a book and those who do not travel read only one page* (St. Augustine). Amen!

If you'd like to know more about me or any of these titles, you can check out www.terrancezepke.com or www.terrancetalkstravel.com. You can also find lengthy descriptions and "look inside" options through most online booksellers. Please note that links to book previews have been included in this booklet for your convenience.

The primary purpose of this guide is to introduce you to some titles you may not have known about. Another reason for it is to let you know all the ways you can connect with me. Authors love to hear from readers. We truly appreciate you more than you'll ever know. Please feel free to send me a comment or question via the comment form found on every page on my websites or follow me on your favorite social media. Don't forget that you can also listen to my writing podcast on iTunes, **A Writer's Journey**, or my travel show, **Terrance Talks Travel: Über Adventures** on Blog Talk Radio and iTunes. The best way to make sure you don't miss any episodes of these shows, new book releases and giveaways, contests, my TRIP PICK OF THE WEEK, cheap travel tips, free downloadable travel reports, my annual Countdown to Halloween (including recipes, party planning tips, and special seasonal events/haunted attractions), and travel trends and news is to subscribe to **Terrance Talks Travel** on www.terrancetalkstravel.com or *A Writer's Journey* or **Mostly Ghostly** on www.terrancezepke.com.

Terrance

See the next page for a sneak peek of

SPOOKIEST LIGHTHOUSES:
Discover America's Most Haunted Lighthouses

New London Ledge Lighthouse

Location: New London (harbor), Connecticut

Built: 1909

Visitor Information: Open to the public.

The light is operational but has been automated since 1986. There is no staff at New London Ledge Lighthouse. During the summer months, tours can be arranged through Project Oceanology (www.oceanology.org). This 2.5-hour tour includes time inside the tower. Area ferries and cruise tours offer views of the lighthouse, but this is the only one that permits inside access. The lighthouse, which is on the National Register of Historic Places, is owned by the US Coast Guard and managed by the New London Ledge Lighthouse Foundation.

About the Haunted Lighthouse: Architectural buffs will note the French and Colonial influences that are prevalent in this unusual-looking beacon. It is a combination Victorian mansion and lighthouse. Interestingly, the crib (made of pine, iron, and steel) was built and then transported to this site using four tugboats. Upon arrival at its new home, the crib was filled with concrete, riprap, and gravel, and then sunk. A concrete pier was built on top of the crib and the tower placed on top of it. Originally, it had a fourth-order Fresnel lens in the lantern room, which illuminated three white flashes followed by one red flash.

It is reportedly haunted by former keeper John "Ernie" Randolph. When Ernie took the assignment, he brought his second wife with him. His new bride was half his age. They were happy—in the beginning. But as time went on, she grew restless and bored—and unhappy and lonely.

One day, while Ernie was out securing supplies, a ferry captain stopped by to check on the couple. The desperate woman threw some belongings in a bag, scribbled a "Dear Ernie" note, and left with the ferry captain. When Ernie returned and read the note from his wife, he became so despondent that he killed himself. That was in 1936.

But it seems that Ernie is still here—and he is a mischievous spirit. He often moves tools and books in the library. He turns the foghorn on. He tidies the place. A keeper's wife, who lived here during the 1940s, saw an apparition she believed was Ernie. Her husband, who wouldn't admit to believing in ghosts, did admit that possessions he kept safeguarded in a locked desk drawer were often rearranged. The couple also reported an unidentifiable fishy odor and cold spots. Others have reported seeing a shadowy figure on occasion.

When Coast Guard crew members were stationed here, they reported knocking on their bedroom doors during the night. The television turned on and off seemingly on its own. Doors often open and close. Floors and windows have been meticulously cleaned, but no one knows by whom. None of the staff takes credit when asked who did the nice job on the windows. But perhaps the spookiest thing was when the covers were pulled off the bed of Coast Guard crew members by an unseen presence. The men admitted they had trouble getting back to sleep after seeing their blankets removed by a ghost. The lighthouse has been featured on the television shows, *Scariest Places on Earth* and *Ghost Hunters*.

Index

Daughters of the American Revolution, 22
Decatur, Illinois, 113, 115
demonology, 154

Eason, Connecticut, 151
Ed Warren, 8, 152, 154
Edgar Allan Poe, 82, 84, 85
El Campo Santo Cemetery, 7, 132, 133, 134
Exeter, Rhode Island, 124, 125, 127
Expedition Unknown, 131

Farnsworth House Inn, 73
Find-a-Grave, 111
Florida, 157
French Quarter, 33, 42

Gallows Hill, 147
Georgia Historical Commission, 26
Gettysburg Address, 75
Gettysburg College, 72
Gettysburg National Military Park Cemetery, 3, 9, 64, 65
Gettysburg, Pennsylvania, 65
Ghost Adventures, 60
Ghost dog, 63
ghost dogs, 101
Ghost Hunters, 190
ghost hunting tours, 115
Ghost Lights, 7, 61, 119

Terrance Zepke

Made in the USA
Coppell, TX
13 July 2022

79913218R00101